Praise for *Shark Sense*

Everyone Needs to Get in Touch with His or Her Inner Shark Sense!

I found this book very inspiring and motivating. I liked the setup of the book; it was a nice, easy read, with very cute pictures and comments throughout, and it still packed a punch in terms of inspiring and motivating content. It's the type of book that, after reading, you feel as if you could do anything, and a book you can always go back to when you are unsure of your plan of action. Sharkie has been there and learned these important life lessons, and you get to use her knowledge to make your life that much better. I would recommend this book to anyone, especially women, because we all need a little shark in us!

—Erica L. Carleton, *The Happy Critic* (Moose Jaw, SK, Canada)

Sharkie Slams One Home

This is a good, quick read with great life lessons tied to how sharks use these lessons to rule the water and their lives. It pumps you up to live your life as you wish and make the best of each day, regardless of what life has dealt you. From yoga camp to professional volleyball to child rearing, she uses excellent real-life examples to help you understand the lessons more vividly. If you want to get refreshed about what life has to offer, read it now and then "go grab life by the horns and show it who's boss." Good job, Sharkie!

—J.J. Wilson, MBA, JD, CMA (Toledo, OH)

Don't Be Shark Bait

Sharkie's story is the basis of this book, encouraging the reader to be like a shark and go after what he or she wants. It's an inspirational book filled with personal accounts and suggestions for the reader to do as the author did in order to reach goals. A quick read—it's an upbeat alternative to the depressing evening news.

—Career Doc (Boston, MA)

The Ball's in Our Court

Sharkie Zartman is a "been there, done that" kind of woman. Long before it was popular, she called upon a male coach to help her develop her volleyball skills. Along the way she not only learned the game but became part of a team and also found the perfect partner to share her life.

This is not Sharkie's first book and hopefully won't be her last. Her easygoing style makes you feel like you're having a conversation with a close friend who truly has your best interests at heart. Young or old, male or female, athlete or simply on the sidelines, this book offers interesting insights to all.

With a series of real-life stories and situations, she lets us know that we're not alone out there, and with a little shark sense we can improve our current state of being. Weight issues, confidence, choices, career paths, and parental insights all get a moment to step up and challenge us. In a simple format of story/situation, how it relates to a shark's sensibilities, and how we can learn to confront these problems, Sharkie guides us through and brings us out on the other side.

—Donna Coomer, *Between the Lines Reviews,* (Hartshorn, MO)

Acting Like a Shark Can Be Good for You

If I had been blessed with a unique name, I'd like to think I could be half as clever as Sharkie Zartman has been in using it to impart self-motivational directives that are effective as well as pertinent to the subject matter. Discovering the truisms of life based on your namesake is a gift that Ms. Zartman shares through personal anecdotes that illustrate shark-like traits. It's doubtful that many people realize they have an inner shark, so they most likely have not gotten in touch with it. But by heeding the advice in Shark Sense, *they'll be able to tap into this potential power of a formidable predator. The shark senses enumerated may seem familiar at first glance, but by melding personal experiences gained as a professional athlete, mother, and teacher, Ms. Zartman casts them in a new light that is uplifting and motivating. The senses overlap many facets of everyday* life—work, health, personal relationships, and inner peace—making this book helpful to a wide audience.

—B. Burke, Reviewer at *Bookpleasures*

The Sharkman

At the moment I have such a huge smile on my face because I have just read Shark Sense *and am amazed at how Sharkie has managed to combine shark and human attributes and hit home with such accuracy. Humans have always feared sharks and labeled them frightening, senseless killers, but the fact is that if humans tried to adapt their style of living to that of these magnificent creatures, our lives would be so much happier and healthier!*

—Alex "The Sharkman" Buttigieg, World Organization (to save and protect sharks), www.sharkmans-world.com

Shark Sense

Shark Sense

Getting in Touch with Your Inner Shark

Sharkie Zartman

iUniverse, Inc.
Bloomington

Shark Sense
Getting in Touch with Your Inner Shark

iUniverse books may be ordered through booksellers or by contacting:

iUniverse
1663 Liberty Drive
Bloomington, IN 47403
www.iuniverse.com
1-800-Authors (1-800-288-4677)

ISBN: 978-1-4502-7740-2 (sc)
ISBN: 978-1-4502-7741-9 (dj)
ISBN: 978-1-4502-7742-6 (ebk)

Library of Congress Control Number: 2010918354

Printed in the United States of America

iUniverse rev. date: 01/17/2011

To my dad, Len, who had the nerve and the wisdom to name me after one of the world's most feared creatures. To him I owe my uniqueness, my drive, and my courage. And yes, Dad, I did my best!

Contents

Foreword

Sharks are winners. They figured out what they wanted to do millions of years ago, learned how to do that efficiently and then continued to improve their game over all these years. Try to get them to settle for less than what they want and you are in for a difficult struggle.

I found out recently just how dangerous a shark can be when you interfere with what they want to do. What I did was just plain stupid, not shark or eco friendly and otherwise dangerous and dumb. I am ashamed to admit that I pulled a good size Nurse shark out from under some coral so my friends could get a good look at him.

Turns out that Nurse sharks are really fast, very flexible and that small looking mouth can take off a hand in a hurry. He was after me in a nano-second. He took a good snap at my hand and just missed renaming me Lefty. At that, he decided he had made his point and swam off calmly. I swam off as well…not so calmly. My buddies in the boat told me I swam away like a ten year old fighting off a swarm of bees.

The "sharks" I've met in the workplace are equally focused on getting what they want out of life. They seem to win by refusing to lose. You can't discourage them, get them to quit or move them off course, until they have accomplished their goals. And some of them are about as dangerous as that innocent looking Nurse shark.

Sharkie Zartman is just that kind of person. With a name like Sharkie, it is not surprising that she grew up to learn from shark behavior. And learn she did. When others told her she was too small to be a big time athlete, she just quietly went on to become a collegiate and USA volleyball All-American, a national champion, a member of our National Volleyball Team and a volleyball professional. When her competitors discounted her because of her size, she just beat them. Having learned my lesson once, I will not be pulling her out from under the coral to show her off to my friends. But I would like to show her off to you. She has written an exceptional book on winning despite the odds, on making your dreams come true and on learning things from shark behavior that will serve you (and me) throughout our lives.

I am inspired by her story of winning despite long odds against her. I am moved by what she has managed to accomplish thus far in her life. But much more importantly, I appreciate the fact that she took the time to put down her ideas on winning in a succinct, witty and enjoyable book.

I wish I had written this book. Of course, my name is Don and her name is Sharkie…so it is probably better that she was the one with the terrific idea to link the lessons learned from nature's longest surviving winners…the sharks…with those practices that can help all of us win in life. **DonnySense** just doesn't grab one's attention like **SharkSense.** This is the second time I have narrowly missed writing a commercially successful book. The other was titled **Donny Potter.** My wife had suggested **"Harry…",** but…no…I insisted on **"Donny…"** My wife has the good shark sense in the family.

As near as I can figure, we only get one life to live. We can live it small and seemingly safe or we can live large and accomplish absolutely anything we set out to achieve. Sharkie chose to live large. She set unreasonably high goals, defied the odds, never let herself get off track and put in the hard work until all of her goals were met. She can give you the insights you need to do the same. Some of the ideas are as old as sharks. And that is not a bad thing. Sharks have been winning for a very long time.

Enjoy the Sharkie sense. I did. And I really do wish I had written this book.

Donald J. Hurzeler

Don is a retired CEO/President of Zurich Middle Markets Insurance Company, former president of the Zurich Foundation and of the Society of Chartered Property and Casualty Underwriters and author of *Designated for Success* and *The Way Up: How to Keep Your Career Moving in the Right Direction*

Acknowledgments

Thanks to my husband, Pat, for seeing me through another writing project. I keep telling him, "This will be the last one," but then I come up with a new idea. He is my best friend, the love of my life, and has the patience of a saint.

A huge thank-you to Bobbi McKenna, a gifted mentor, for her support, guidance and expertise in making this book a reality. I also wish to thank Rosalie Mervosh at Creative Juices for designing many of the shark graphics used throughout the book.

Several people offered advice while I was developing the book, including George Murphy, Keely Sims, Heather Hall, and Holly McPeak. Also, special thanks to Alex Buttigieg, "The Sharkman," who reviewed the manuscript and contributed information on sharks.

A special thanks to my wonderful daughters, who have gone through life with a mom named after a killer fish. They have been a joy to raise and have been troopers in life. I am so proud to be their mother.

Sincere thanks to all of these fine people.

Introduction

Yell the word "shark!" and you will get a heightened automatic response, especially if you are near a body of water. I should know because my name is Sharkie. Even though "Charleen" is on my birth certificate, I have been called "Sharkie" my whole life. My dad must have seen something in my eyes to know that this strange nickname would be a good match for me.

Being named after a predator fish has been an interesting experience. When I was little, I was often nervous when introduced to people for the first time. They would get strange looks on their faces, take a couple of steps backward, or ask me to repeat my name because they thought they heard it wrong. One thing is for sure—they never forgot my name!

Why are these amazing creatures so frightening and interesting? Sharks have always been somewhat of a mystery to humans, especially since they do not communicate with us. There is no such thing as a shark whisperer. Even so, we have ultimate respect for them, particularly when we venture into their territory.

In the ocean, sharks are at the top of the food chain and swim about with confidence and purpose. They are true to their nature. Sharks do not have divided minds, and they do not experience self-doubt. Emotions, competition, expectations, and judgments do not bog them down. They don't depend on anyone else for survival or expect life to be fair.

Can we say the same for us? Is there anything we can learn from sharks to help us reach our goals? We respect them; they fascinate us;

and we are scared to death of them. When you go into the ocean, do you ever get nervous when you see a large shadow approaching you in the water? Are you any match for a shark?

Shark Sense is about learning to use our instinctive wisdom to supplement logic. We all have an inner shark waiting to emerge. It is a powerful, simple, no-nonsense approach to life. Unfortunately, humans are notorious for making easy things hard, multitasking, and seeking answers outside of themselves instead of looking inward.

The brain of a shark is small compared to ours. Even the average white shark's brain weighs about 1.2 ounces, whereas an average human brain weighs 48 ounces. Scientists have said for a long time that we use less than 10 percent of our brain's capacity. Could it be that the unused part of our brain turns out to be the simplest to access?

As a professor, coach, and former All-American athlete, I am confident the following *Shark Sense* principles work. They are timeless, true, and simple. Countless coaches, athletes, business experts, and self-help gurus have long utilized these principles. Using the shark as an example makes them even simpler to understand and utilize. Discover these qualities in yourself, utilize them, and your life will change for the better.

Are you ready to dive in?

Shark Sense One:
A Shark Is Always True to Its Nature

Human Translation:
Know Who You Are and What You Want

The shark came slowly, steadily, as if it had no need for speed, for it knew it could not be stopped.—Peter Benchley

It was a hot August afternoon in Southern California, and the air was dry and heavy, making it difficult to breathe. The sand was blistering hot except down by the water, where everyone was hanging out. I was eight years old on a beach outing with my family, waist-deep in the water, jumping and diving through the waves with the other bathers, swimmers, and surfers. It was getting late, and my parents started to pack up the cooler and towels. I turned my back, ignored them, and kept jumping the waves. I didn't want to leave.

My sister started to yell at me from the shore. "Sharkie, Shark! It's time to go!" She kept yelling my name, and I ignored her, hoping she would go away. I'll never forget what happened next. Suddenly, everyone in my near vicinity ran out of the water in a panic. All around me people were splashing, screaming, and sprinting for the sand. At first I didn't understand what was happening, but then I realized that all those people thought there was a real shark in the water. No, it was just me ignoring my sister as usual.

I never really thought that much about sharks until I saw the movie *Jaws* and, like so many others, was terrified to go swimming in the ocean afterward. I couldn't believe my dad named me after such a horrible, mean, ugly fish. No wonder people reacted so strongly to my name. I knew my name was different, but after *Jaws* I realized it was downright scary!

Now, after many years, I realize there is more to a shark than what Hollywood wants us to believe. Even Peter Benchley, the creator of Jaws, took a different perspective on these amazing creatures in his book, *Shark Life*. He explained:

> I am now convinced that attacks on human beings which I had thought were intentional, were mostly cases of mistaken identity. Sharks had been condemned as man-eaters for thousands of years, and it would be several more years before that belief would be effectively challenged. We knew so little back then and have learned so much since; I couldn't possibly write the same story today. I know now that the mythic monster I created was largely fiction (Benchley 2005).

Mr. Benchley stopped writing about rogue monster sharks and instead became involved in shark conservation up to his death in 2006. He strived to change their image from mindless killers to essential creatures that are a necessary part of the ocean's ecological balance.

While it is true that sharks are predators and on rare occasions attack humans, less than ten people per year die from shark incidents, whereas around 150 die from being hit by falling coconuts. Maybe we need to be more concerned about coconuts. Also, out of more than 350 known species of sharks, 80 percent do not hurt people (Pope 2002). By far, the most shocking statistic is that for every human killed by a shark attack, there are roughly ten million sharks killed by humans, mostly for their fins, flesh, skins, teeth, cartilage, and organs (Benchley 2005). Many sharks are now hunted for their dorsal fins alone, which are cut off the sharks immediately after they are caught and used as an exotic soup ingredient. Then the sharks are thrown back into the water, defenseless, to bleed to death or be eaten by other sharks.

Who are the real monsters?

Sharks have been on this earth for over four hundred million years, predating even the dinosaurs (Kalman 2003). They have survived the harshest environmental conditions and have adapted in order to survive. Sharks are efficient at what they are programmed to do: swim, eat, and make little sharks. Their purpose is to maintain the balance of nature in the ocean, and they accomplish this by being perfectly designed eating machines. If they were not a part of the ocean environment, its ecological balance would be severely compromised. Sharks are genuine and goal-oriented, use their strengths, and are not even aware of their weaknesses. It's easy to understand why they are at the top of the food chain in the ocean.

When humans venture into the ocean, we are in their territory, and everything in the water is considered food—including us! As Peter Benchlely eventually recognized--*we are the aliens in the water.* We wouldn't venture into the jungle in the middle of the Amazon without considering that there are some animals, snakes, and insects that most likely don't appreciate our presence or might do us harm. So why do we go into the ocean and feel as though we own the place and not take precautions? Instead of being arrogant or downright stupid, why can't we respect other forms of life on the planet and their environments and realize that all living beings have a reason for being here?

The first time I remember using my *Shark Sense* was when I was three years old. We were living in Lubbock, Texas, close to the air force base. My parents took me and my sister to the park, and we were headed for the swings when something caught my eye. It was an American flag waving in the breeze at the top of a long pole.

My parents took their eyes off me for a second, and when they turned around, I was off sprinting toward the flag. Before they could stop me, I was halfway up the pole, going for the top. All they could see were my diapered behind and my skinny legs moving upward. I could hear my parents pleading from below, "Please, Sharkie, come down, slowly!"

Funny, I don't think I had ever heard them say "please" to me before, but I do remember hearing "no" quite often.

I made it to the top of the pole and grabbed the flag with my chubby hands. It wouldn't budge, and I started to throw a mini-tantrum. But then I looked down and saw the view from the top. I didn't feel scared because it was amazing seeing everything look so small, and I felt so big! I wanted to stay there forever, but from below I could hear my mom crying hysterically, so I slowly shimmied down the pole.

My parents were so relieved that I made it down unscathed that they didn't get mad at me. I also learned an important principle: where there's a will, there's a way. I never went up that pole again, but I knew I could do it if I really wanted to.

What's your flag? We all have at least one goal or dream tugging at us that wants to be realized. We also have a reason for being here or a purpose. What is it for you right now? Are you considering a new career or searching for a special person to share your life? How about optimal health or financial security? Do you have a desire to do something with your life that is unconventional or different from what you are doing now?

To complement any goal or purpose, we have well-equipped, goal-oriented instincts, especially when we are very young. This is what I call our *inner shark*. Just ask your parents what you were like when you were two or three years old. I'll bet you were inquisitive, adventurous, and didn't have any fears. As a parent, I realize we cannot allow our kids to run around like unsupervised little sharks. We need to set boundaries to keep them from getting hurt, destroying property, or worse.

As children grow up, their parents' voices are replaced by an inner voice of caution, doom, and gloom that sends messages like: Be careful; Don't take a chance, you might make a mistake; or You will be sorry! That original sense of fire, determination, and freedom gets snuffed out. We submerge our sense of self and try to fit into our families, society, culture, religion, and schools. In an effort to fit in and feel loved, we lose a genuine part of ourselves. Some of our natural talents become suppressed because they were considered unworthy or unimportant by others whom we valued. In other words, the inner shark is no longer working for us because we have put it to sleep.

Eventually, our lives become cluttered with chores and responsibilities. We're more concerned with paying bills and making others happy than living our own lives. One day we wake up and realize we are making everyone happy but ourselves. What you really want in your life becomes a hard question to answer because you haven't asked the question in such a long time. So I encourage you to ask it now. What do you want? Only then will the inner shark in you awaken.

> *When you have determined what you want, you have made the most important decision in your life. You have to know what you want in order to attain it.—Douglas Lurtan*

A while back I attended a workshop on weight loss and nutrition where the guest lecturers were sharing secrets on how to help people lose weight. Most of the speakers were talking about the latest workout regiments, gimmicks, or supplements. They all started to sound alike; however, I'll never forget one speaker. He said the unthinkable: "If you want to lose weight, take off all your clothes, look in the mirror, and tell yourself that you are responsible for this."

The message was not well received. The audience started to boo the speaker, and some even threw their food at him. They tried to "kill the messenger." As he collected himself, he proceeded to explain that unless we take responsibility for the choices that got us where we are today, we will never change. It will always be easier to blame others or make someone else responsible for our lives.

This nugget of wisdom is essential for anyone who wants to achieve a goal. Where am I now? How did I get here? What choices did I make that got me here? Where do I want to go from here? What can I do differently now? Possessing the courage to look inside ourselves, taking responsibility for our past behaviors, igniting the desire to change, and realizing that the only limits are the ones we impose on ourselves, is imperative to changing our lives for the better. We need to accept where we are today and know that only our behaviors will change us! That is where the authenticity comes in. We must not lie to ourselves. Accountability and responsibility generate self-esteem. The more authentic we are, the more powerful we become and once again, the inner shark can emerge, thrive, and move us toward our goals.

As the late John Wooden used to say: "If we are not true to ourselves, we cannot be true to others—our wife or husband, our family, our profession and colleagues" (Wooden 1997).

By now you are probably wondering why I am comparing human behaviors to shark behaviors. What's the point? We're human and sharks are fish. However, as we look closer at some of the sharks' attributes, there is a great deal to learn from their simplicity, focus, and persistence. Why not take a look at what makes them successful instead of fearing them or trying to wipe them off the face of the planet for some exotic soup?

Shark Action Steps

1. Take fifteen minutes each day to get away from your environment. Spend the time alone without distractions. Ask yourself the question: "What do I really want?" If nothing comes to mind, then ask: "How may I make a difference in this life?"

2. If you knew you only had one year to live, would you still be doing what you are now?

3. Identify at least ten goals you would like to achieve before you die.

4. Write them down!

5. Which one has the highest urgency?

6. Once you identify a primary objective, list your personal strengths that will facilitate reaching this goal.

7. What will slow you down? Identify the people or the conditions that are barriers to your success.

8. Put a target date on this goal. When would you like it to be realized?

9. Identify the tasks you need to complete before this goal is achieved.

10. Commit to performing at least three tasks a day.

11. Schedule these tasks as you would any other priority.

12. How will achieving this goal change your life? Write down anything that occurs to you.

Quotes on Goal-Seeking Behaviors:

Shoot for the moon. Even if you miss, you'll land among the stars.
—Les Brown

I can't change the direction of the wind, but I can adjust my sails to always reach my destination.—Jimmy Dean

If you don't know where you are going, you will probably end up somewhere else.—Lawrence J. Peter

There is no passion to be found in playing small; in settling for a life that is less than the one you are capable of living.—Nelson Mandela

Goals are the fuel in the furnace of achievement.—Brian Tracy

There is a law in psychology that if you form a picture in your mind of what you would like to be, and you keep and hold that picture there long enough, you will soon become exactly as you have been thinking.—William James

The greater danger for most of us is not that our aim is too high and we miss it, but that it is too low and we reach it.—Michelangelo

Shark Sense Two:
Sharks Don't Ask for Permission

Human Translation:
Be Independent of Others' Opinions

Do not become too concerned about what others may think of you. Be very concerned about what you think of yourself. Too often we care more about a stranger's opinion of us than our own.—John Wooden

When I was seventeen years old, my dream was to be a great volleyball player. My days were filled with running along the beach and going from court to court looking for games. I played with and against anyone who would let me on the court.

One day my high school coach called me into her office. I thought that she was going to compliment me since I threw my body into the wall to get a ball during practice. But instead of the praise I'd been expecting, she said: "Sharkie, I think you should quit volleyball." She looked stern and serious. She went on to explain that I was too short, uncoordinated, and out of control to ever be any good at volleyball. I was crushed! I knew my volleyball skills were less than impressive, but I was not ready to quit my passion, even though my coach thought it was in my best interest. The fact that she said I should quit made me want it even more. It was my starting gun and activated my inner shark.

I became obsessed with finding someone who would help me become a better player. I wasn't going to get better on my own, and my high school coach certainly wasn't going to help. It seemed hopeless since most girls did not pursue sports, especially after high school. The chances of playing in college were slim. But I wasn't ready to give up. I soon found out that one of the football coaches at our school was also a volleyball player and coached a men's club volleyball team. He had a reputation of being strict, disciplined, and mysterious as well. Coach Z was his name, and all the football players were afraid of him. Desperate, I walked into his office and asked if he would help me become a great volleyball player since my high school coach had given my volleyball career a death sentence. I'll never forget his strange buzz haircut.

After hearing all the stories about how mean he was to the football players, I started to get nervous thinking that maybe this was a bad idea. But something in his eyes told me that he was the one who could help. He said that he would coach me if I got enough girls to form a team. No problem.

I recruited girls who were marginal players and had little volleyball experience. We even had a girl who would scream and duck every time someone would hit a ball toward her. Needless to say, our first year was a disaster. My new coach had never trained girls before, so it was also an education for him. He learned quickly about PMS, boyfriend problems, and girly gossip. Coaching girls was a whole new ballgame! But my new mentor persevered. The next year, we started to win matches, and the other teams stopped laughing at us. In fact, a few teams were afraid to play us. Eventually, our team attracted some of the finest athletes in the game, and we won the USVBA national title and beat the top-seeded Adidas team in the finals. Their coach was so upset when they lost to us that he threatened to go back to Japan!

I was recruited to play volleyball at UCLA and was on the first national championship team. Playing volleyball quickly became the focal point of my life as I continued to play both college and club ball. Being selected for the World University Team and the US National Team was the high point of my indoor career. Whenever I saw our flag and heard the national anthem, it sent chills up my spine. I was representing my country and playing against the best volleyball teams in the world.

The best part of this story is that I found the love of my life on this volleyball journey. Eight years after I met my new coach—the football coach with the buzz haircut—I married him. Do you think I would have found him if I had listened to my high school coach and given up on my dream? I don't think so. Knowing what I wanted and not being slowed down by people who were unsupportive opened up a whole new life for me.

No approval or permission is required in the shark world. They simply do what they know is right for them. No exceptions; no hesitation; no need to listen to others' advice. There are no shark meetings being held under the water that empower some and not others. They see their world through their eyes only, and that's enough for them to be successful. They swim right past their detractors and nobody slows them down.

Sharks are autonomous from birth. A baby shark (pup) must make a quick exit away from the mother after birth, or it may just become her next meal. Baby sharks must take care of themselves. They do not get to be nursed or receive love and affection. Their parents are nowhere to be found right after they are born. Talk about being self-sufficient!

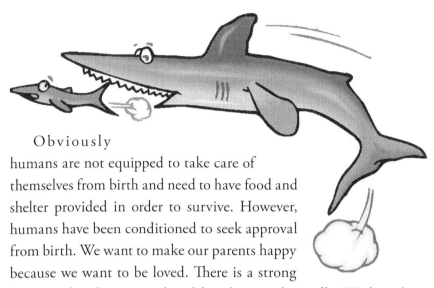

Obviously humans are not equipped to take care of themselves from birth and need to have food and shelter provided in order to survive. However, humans have been conditioned to seek approval from birth. We want to make our parents happy because we want to be loved. There is a strong basic need to be accepted and loved unconditionally. We have been raised to satisfy others and follow rules. Some of us even develop an all-too-common *disease to please*. Richard Machowicz, former Navy SEAL and author of *Unleashing the Warrior Within*, elaborates on this issue:

> Stop looking to others to give you permission to go after the target you want to knock down. You are your own master. Set the target up, and then knock it down. It really is that simple once you stop waiting for permission. Stop waiting for the perfect moment. Stop waiting until you can move perfectly. Stop saying you'd do it if only you had a sharper weapon. Stop waiting for the ideal situation. There is no such thing (Machowicz 2000).

As we grow older, there is nothing wrong with wanting others to accept our lives or give us their approval. We just don't *need* it! After all, no one sees the world the way we do or knows what is in our hearts. According to the famous psychologist Abraham Maslow, the highest place a human can achieve on the road to self-actualization is to be above the need for others' approval. How true! Only then can we go out and make an impact on the world—like a shark. If we suppress our feelings and always put others' opinions first, we are ignoring our own instincts and are likely to give up or get discouraged.

Donald Hurzeler, CPCU, CLU. is a retired CEO/President of Zurich Middle Markets Insurance Company, former president of the Zurich Foundation and of the Society of Chartered Property and Casualty Underwriters and author of *Designated for Success*. In this book he lists what he calls weapons of mass destruction developed by society to discourage a man or woman from being a powerful force in this world. People using these weapons will:

- Make you feel guilty for your success.
- Make you feel guilty or silly for even wanting to be successful.
- Talk behind your back.
- Shun you.
- Tell you, "You can't."
- Tell you that it has already been tried with disastrous results.
- Ask you, "Why would you want to do that?"
- Make fun of you.
- Post nasty notes on the Internet about you.
- Talk to the press about you.
- Try to sabotage your efforts.
- Celebrate your defeats.
- Ridicule you.
- Ignore your success.
- Attribute your success to "being lucky."
- Steal credit from you.
- Try to knock you off your course.
- Discourage you.
- Spit on your dreams.
- Lay traps for you.

○ Beat you when you are down.[1]

As you can see, there are many tactics used by people out there who don't want you to succeed. Misery apparently enjoys company. If you are successful, in their minds, it might make them look bad or put the pressure on them to do something other than sit on their behinds. There will always be critics in the world who will tell you all the reasons why you should not try a new venture. It's almost as if they have a master's degree in dream smashing. Don't listen. If it's important enough to you, there are people out there who will help you. You just have to find them!

Pete Carroll, the former USC football guru and current NFL coach, understands his role as it relates to his athletes. In his new book, *Win Forever,* he talks about when he first started to develop his own coaching philosophy:

> What if my job as a coach isn't so much to force or coerce performance as it is to create situations where players develop the confidence to set their talents free and pursue their potential to its full extent? What if my job as a coach is really to prove to these kids how good they already are, and how good they could possibly become, and that they are truly capable of high-level performance (Carroll 2010)?

Obviously, Pete Carroll was successful because he is one of those few people who knows and understands the potential in each individual, and instead of destroying dreams, he helps to manifest them.

We have two daughters, Teri and Chrissie, who love volleyball and are also "vertically challenged." Many "experts" in the sport advised them to give up on their desires to play in college because they were too short. But, like their mom, they became more determined. Both girls

---

1   Used with permission from Donald J. Hurzeler, *Designated for Success,* 55-56.

received full athletic scholarships to college. Teri went to University of California at Irvine and was the assist leader for setters, and Chrissie went to UCLA, where she was named a Division 1 All-American.

Both my daughters still play in tournaments on the beach. In fact, I was playing with Teri a while back in a tournament, and a woman approached me. She said: "You remind me of a girl who used to play a long time ago. Her name was Sharkie. Are you related to her?" I thought she was kidding. I said: "Yes, I am Sharkie." She looked at me in disbelief. She couldn't believe I was still playing after all these years. But I'm not ready to give up playing just yet. Sharks keep swimming until they die, and I'll keep going too, as long as my knees hold up. I know who I am and what I want. No one will stop me. I don't need anyone's approval, and neither do you.

Shark Action Steps

1. List the people in your life who intimidate you or stomp on your dreams.

2. Why are these people's opinions so important to you? Are they really valid experts?

3. What would happen if you ignored their advice?

4. What would be the worst thing that could happen if you decided to go after your top goal?

5. How will you feel if you don't try to attain this dream? Will you have regrets later?

6. How could your life improve if you achieved this goal?

7. Are you ready to swim past the naysayers?

Quotes on Independence

If a man does not keep pace with his companions, perhaps it is because he hears a different drummer. Let him step to the music which he hears, however measured and far away.—Henry David Thoreau

When you are inspired by some great purpose, some extraordinary project, all your thoughts break their bonds; your mind transcends limitations, your consciousness expands in every direction, and you find yourself in a new, great and wonderful world. Dormant forces, faculties and talents become alive, and you discover yourself to be a greater person by far than you ever dreamed yourself to be.—Patanjali

Pay no attention to what the critics say. A statue has never been erected in honor of a critic.—Jean Sibelius

Shark Sense Three:
Sharks Swim Forward

Human Translation: Action Is the Key to Success

Action may not always bring happiness; but there is no happiness without action.—Benjamin Disraeli

Wishing, hoping, thinking, and planning will never get you anywhere until you take action. I've seen countless people plan a perfect life and never live it because they were afraid to move out of their perceived comfort zone. We are not magnets that attract success. If we want success, we must move toward it—*we must take action*. Sharks do not wait for food to come to them; instead they are always moving forward toward their goals. They also don't live in the past and make themselves sick over the ones that got away. They live in the present moment, always moving forward and never looking back. How different would our lives be if we adopted this philosophy?

A while back, my best friend had just moved to Missouri, and I wanted to go visit her. However, it was summer and our teaching funds were limited. Coincidentally, there was a beach volleyball tournament scheduled the weekend before I wanted to leave, and the prize money for the winning team was just enough to pay for my trip. The only problem was that Gregory and McFadden, who at the time were considered the best beach doubles team in the country, were planning to play in this one. Winning a tournament in those days was almost impossible if this team was entered, because they were aggressive, confident, and one of the players was great at harassing her opponents.

I must admit, in the past, I used to let Gregory's antics get to me.—most everyone did. She was, in her own words, "colorful" and would cackle and scream when she dug your hardest spikes. "What else you got?" was one of her favorite taunts. "My grandmother could have dug that ball!" was another. She tried to get into your head and was very good at it. I had never beaten her before—but this was a new day.

During the finals, I was so focused, I didn't hear her comments. It didn't matter that they had won all those tournaments in the past. The only thing that mattered to me was winning this tournament so I could see my friend. I was playing in the present moment and not even aware of the crowd or the other team.

We accomplished the unthinkable and won the tournament. I remember Gregory storming off the court after the final match, mumbling all the way to the ocean. I hugged my partner and family members and immediately began searching for a phone to make my airline reservations. I was stoked! I was going to Missouri!

When I think back, I realize my mindset was very different than in past tournaments. I was more in tune with what was happening on each contact with the ball than ever before. The desire to attain a new goal and the opportunity to get it almost immediately set something in motion. Present-moment awareness is a powerful tool to utilize to propel movement toward any goal. Never reverting backward and always moving forward while keeping your awareness in the present is what makes success attainable. The shark is a perfect example of how simple this mindset is. If a shark is approaching you in the water, chances are he is not thinking about the past but instead is very focused on the present moment and his ultimate goal, which hopefully is not you.

Sharks don't back down and cower before other creatures. They have been known to attack prey much bigger than themselves, including boats. All their motions are deliberate. They do not react to their environment or get rattled or distracted. Sharks respond to any challenges in the moment with all they have. Sharks never come to a fast stop or swim backward. Except when resting (with their eyes open), they are in constant motion. In fact, in 2005, a white shark tagged in South Africa completed the first known transoceanic trip for an individual shark, traveling more than 13,670 miles to the coast of Australia and back again. They don't stay put. And neither should we.

Taking action is the key to making our dreams come true. Oliver Wendell Holmes once said: "The great thing in this world is not so much where you stand, but in what direction you are moving" (Hurzeler

2004). Nothing happens in a state of inertia. Most of us know what we need to do to get what we want. If it is an athletic goal, we need to train and improve our skills and concentration. If it is a job, we can acquire appropriate training and experience. If we want to change our health, we have to change our habits. We cannot sit and expect people and situations to change for us. Analyzing, dreaming, and hoping that our lives will improve doesn't work. Taking action is always the most important part of achieving results. It is the bridge between the dream and the goal.

Sylvester Stallone, creator of *Rocky* and star of countless movies, realizes the power of action. He says: "I'm not the smartest or most talented person in the world, but I succeed because I keep going, and going and going." His recent movie, *The Expendables*, debuted as the number one movie in American and Canadian theaters according to Hollywood.com, taking in over $35 million dollars in the opening weekend. Obviously you can't stop him because he has succeeded, failed, succeeded, failed, and succeeded so many times. He just keeps on going and doesn't really care what his detractors have to say.

My daughter Teri has always been a forward thinker. If you put something in her path to block her dreams, she will find a way around it. I remember when she was first starting to mature. All of her friends were getting their first training bras, and she asked me if she could get one too. She had already chosen the bra and the store where she wanted to buy it. "But, sweetie, you don't need a bra yet," I said. She looked at me with a disappointed frown and stared at my chest and said, "You don't need one either, and you have a lot of them!"

Needless to say, she got her bra. Offense versus defense—which one is the most important when we are going after a desired goal? From my daughter's example, it's always offense. We must take action. It's the difference between being a winner and being a victim. Victims allow life to happen to them; winners create their lives with their actions. They are always moving forward.

Besides inaction and the lack of accountability, there is also a tendency for people to stay attached to the past. Sometimes we choose to relive *happy days* over and over again. Other times, we choose to hang on to negative events and can build enough resentment to affect every waking moment.

I once did a visualization exercise in my yoga class at the college. During the final relaxation, I asked my students to imagine a situation with a person where forgiveness and letting go of a past event might help improve the quality of their lives. After class a student approached me. She always stayed in the back of the room and never said a word. She had a rather spooky look about her. But now, she got right in my face and started yelling at me. "What if you can't forgive a person?" She looked like she wanted to kill me. "What then?"

I was taken aback, not ready for a confrontation like this. Then I collected myself and told her that she didn't have to forgive anyone. It was her choice. However, if she did decide to forgive it would be a gift she could give to herself. It would free her from resentment, which was like an anchor in her life, holding her back, pulling her down. The other person didn't even have to know that she had forgiven him or her. I had no idea who the other person was, or what had been done to her. As it was none of my business, I didn't ask.

I didn't see that student again for a couple of weeks, and I figured she resented me for doing the visualization. Finally, she came back to class, and I almost did not recognize her. Her skin was glowing, she was smiling, and her posture exuded confidence. After class, she took me aside and gave me a big hug. "Thank you," she said in a soft voice. "You did for me what years of therapy and medication were not able to do. I never realized it could be so simple."

Byron Katie offers the world a simple process to find joy and let go of the past. Examining our past beliefs and letting go of the ones that no longer serve us offers a powerful turnaround and allows us to experience the opposite of what we believe. This process of inquiry is called The Work and involves four simple questions:

1. Is it true?

2. Can you absolutely know that it's true?

3. How do you react when you believe that thought?

4. Who would you be without the thought?

(Katie 2007)

Simplicity is always underrated. As humans we pride ourselves on being complex creatures. But sometimes our complexities prevent us from living the lives we want. Beliefs and emotions can cloud reality and make life complicated. Keeping things simple, moving forward, and taking action will always push us toward a greater life as long as the goal is a positive outcome. Blaming, living in the past, worrying, rationalizing, and making excuses will only keep us stuck. In order to be free, we must let go of the past, release any fear, and refuse to entertain old pain.

The quicker we let go of old beliefs that no longer serve us, the sooner our lives will change for the better. The energy it takes to hang on to the past holds us back from living a new life. When we change our limiting beliefs, we change our actions and advance forward—like the powerful shark.

Shark Action Steps

1. What past belief(s) may be stopping you from progressing?

2. What is the payoff for you to hold on to this belief?

3. What is the price you have paid to keep this belief alive?

4. Is this belief truly coming from you or is it from someone else?

5. How would your life be different if you let go of this limiting belief?

6. Are you ready to "clean the slate" and move on?

Action Quotes

I have learned that if one advances confidently in the direction of his dreams and endeavors to live the life which he has imagined, he will meet with a success unexpected in common hours.—Henry David Thoreau

An idea not coupled with action will never get any bigger than the brain cell it occupied.—Arnold Glasow

Inaction breeds doubt and fear. Action breeds confidence and courage.—Dale Carnegie

An ounce of action is worth a ton of theory.—Ralph Waldo Emerson

Action is the real measure of intelligence.—Napoleon Hill

You see, in life, lots of people know what to do, but few people actually do what they know. Knowing is not enough! You must take action.—Anthony Robbins

Action is the antidote to despair.—Joan Baez

Great thoughts speak only to the thoughtful mind, but great actions speak to all mankind.—Theodore Roosevelt

The dreams I only thought about, the ones I took no action on, well they are still dreams. But the ones that I took action on, they are now a reality.—Catherine Pulsifer

The superior man is modest in his speech, but exceeds in his actions.—Confucius

Shark Sense Four:
Sharks Do Not Have Divided Minds

Human Translation: Focus on One Goal at a Time

Where attention goes, energy flows and results show.—T. Harv Eker

It should be no surprise to you that what you focus on expands. If you focus on one goal at a time, all your energy will be directed and the chances of success are increased tremendously. However, if you have several goals and try to achieve them all at the same time, the chance of success is diminished significantly. It's not until you risk it all and go for the thing you really want that life becomes unlimited.

Imagine what would happen if we only had one thing to accomplish and there was no time limit. Do you think we would be successful? Would it be worth it? As busy beings, we try to do too many things at once: work, school, relationships, and all sorts of other demands that tug at our energy stores.

We have also become too available and have too many distractions. With cell phones, call waiting, texting, and the Internet, we are constantly being interrupted and bombarded with information. Our energy is being siphoned off in too many directions to have any power. It's similar to putting one gallon of gas into twenty engines. As a result, it's hard to get anywhere—especially if it is a big, juicy goal that takes a heap load of fuel!

Why not put most of the gas into one engine and see how far it takes us? Even if we don't get exactly what we pursued, knowing that we gave it our best shot is an accomplishment in itself. Vince Lombardi, a famous and successful football coach, said it best: "I firmly believe that any man's finest hour—his greatest fulfillment to all he holds dear—is that moment when he has worked his heart out in a good cause and lies exhausted on the field of battle—victorious" (Lombardi 1992).

When a shark is pursuing a goal, it ignores everything else and stays focused on its target. It is honed in. Nothing else matters. It does not allow itself to be distracted and will swim past other prey to get what it wants. Sharks' minds are not divided, and they most assuredly are not into multi-tasking. Sharks are efficient, specialized hunters that have thrived for millions of years. Most of the time, the shark succeeds. It is focused on the task at hand, nothing else, and always goes for the goal.

A while back I had an opportunity to completely submerge myself in a task. It was August, school was starting in a week, and I was going to teach yoga for the first time ever that fall. There was a great deal of pressure to fill the classes and teach them well or the whole program would be scrapped. Even though I was certified to teach yoga and had been doing yoga for my own self-improvement, I still felt that I needed more training because the classes were full and the pressure was intense.

Luckily, a one-week yoga workshop in a resort near Talum, Mexico, was being offered just prior to the start of the semester. The brochure said that at the end of the week, you would come back a different person. It all sounded too good to be true! A whole uninterrupted week of yoga in paradise! The only phrase I was concerned about was *boot camp*. But this was yoga. Just how hard could it possibly be?

As usual, I found out the hard way. The resort was unlike any place I had ever seen before. It was no paradise. There were huts with straw roofs in a jungle-like area on a beach, but that's where the ambiance ended. When I arrived there wasn't time to check in, because the first yoga class was in session. The outside air was getting heavy, and my clothes were drenched in sweat. Was there any chance that this big hut would have cool air?

Unfortunately, it was even hotter inside. The class had already started, and there were over sixty people positioned an inch away from one another on their mats. Several of them glanced at me as I sneaked in and tried to find a spot on the floor. I was wearing the same clothes I had worn on the plane. Have you ever tried to do yoga in jeans? (I do not recommend it.) The introductory class lasted two hours. *Welcome to yoga boot camp.* The orientation was next, where our facilitators reviewed the rules:

#1 Go to all the classes.
#2 Don't complain.
#3 Don't drink the water (it was yellow).
#4 Don't travel anywhere at night.
#5 Don't leave food in your hut.
#6 Leave the animals alone.
What animals? I thought.

The first meal was buffet–style, and usually I can find something edible and tasty in a buffet. As the line kept moving past all the interesting choices, I kept asking myself, *What is this stuff?* Then I remembered the small print in the brochure. We were being fed a mucus-free detox diet for a whole week: no milk products, no meat, no caffeine, no processed foods, no alcohol, no sugar, salt, or bread. Not only was I concerned about sweating to death, now I was worried about how my body was going to handle this radical change of food. Could I possibly get through all this in one week and not die?

There were no mirrors in the resort, so I hadn't noticed that my lips were sunburned and that the humidity and heat had caused them to swell three times their normal size. People were looking at my mouth curiously, probably wondering what whacked-out cosmetic procedure I had endured. This week in "paradise" became the biggest challenge of my life. Not only did my lips hurt, I had a terrible headache, never stopped sweating, and my body was sore all over. My arms also felt like they were going to fall off.

It didn't take long for insecurities to begin to surface. What was I thinking? I was a middle-aged volleyball player trying to keep up with a bunch of experienced yoga fanatics. Was I crazy? Each day, the yoga sessions got harder and harder. Not only did we have to physically *practice* the yoga for ten hours a day—we also had to teach various segments. Our instructor would call out one of our names at any time during the practice and expect whoever was called to lead the class. It was scary. I was being challenged in every way possible.

One night, after sixteen hours of yoga fun, my roommate asked if I would walk down with her on the dirt road so she could call her son, since all the phones were down at the resort. She remembered seeing a pay phone at the end of the road. I reminded her that we weren't supposed to travel at night. (I remembered the rules!) She persisted, so we put on our backpacks and snuck out. The only light we had was one flashlight and the lightening from an approaching storm. We went arm in arm, stepping carefully and slowly along the path. Small animals crossed in front of us, and we recognized most of them as geckos. We had some of their friends as roommates in our hut.

Finally, we saw the phone in the distance with a dim light on top. My roommate called her son, and I was on the lookout. All of a sudden, she started to scream hysterically. I turned and could see that she was covered from head to toe with *bugs*! They were all shapes and sizes. Some had wings and some had big bodies. I couldn't even see her face. Luckily,

I had insect repellent in my backpack. It took me a few seconds to find it, which seemed like an eternity. I sprayed her all over. Then the critters jumped on me. We started fighting over the can of bug spray, trying to spray each other. Finally, I yelled, "Get out of the light!"

We threw ourselves along the side of the road and kept spraying, rolling, and smacking each other to get every last bug off! Finally, exhausted and covered in dirt, we started laughing hysterically. I guess this is why you don't travel the dirt road at night. On the way back to the resort it began raining and the wind picked up. The rain and cool air felt good on our newly bitten skin. We made a pact. No matter what, we would see each other through the rest of the week.

The next morning, we soaked ourselves in tea tree oil and went to class covered with bites. I counted about three hundred on me and even more on her. At least people were no longer looking at my swollen lips. Even though the itching was horrendous, the yoga was becoming easier, and my sore body was starting to feel strong. The week was almost over. Going back to school was becoming a welcome event.

I graduated from yoga boot camp and came back a different person, just like the brochure said I would. I lost over ten pounds that week and was still covered in bites. My colleagues almost didn't recognize me, but I felt confident and achieved a goal in a very short time. No more insecurity for me! I could teach yoga in my sleep.

Focusing on one goal at a time works wonders. At the boot camp, there was nothing for me to do but focus on yoga and surviving. Perhaps I could have gone somewhere less exotic and certainly less intense, but I will never forget my experience. Putting most of our energy into one goal at a time works wonders if you are willing to put in the time and effort. Most of the time people who are unsuccessful are focusing on the problems instead of a goal. Imagine what would happen if they could just reverse their thinking. The mind generally focuses on one predominate thing at a time, so we have a choice as to whether we want to spend our time and energy planning and strategizing for success or whining and complaining about what isn't working.

Also, the harder the challenge is, the more you learn and the greater the reward. Ask any athlete about the best game he ever had. It wasn't the accomplishment of winning—usually it was the fact that it was challenging and the person put everything he had into the effort. As Howard E. Ferguson says in *The Edge*:

> The main reason to go after tough competition is to test you. But there are good reasons: the better the competition, the better the performance; the tougher the competition, the greater the incentive to practice; the greater the competition, the more fun the contest; the tougher the competition, the more motivated you'll be to excel; the greater the competition, the more excited you'll be; the better the competition, the stronger you'll become mentally; and the tougher the competition, the sweeter the victory (Ferguson 1983).

Shark Action Steps

1. Get a planner.

2. How many priorities are demanding your energy now? List them.

3. Schedule out your day and notice where you have time available to put toward your most passionate goal, or one that is coming right up!

4. Commit to the time.

5. Notice how much time you waste in your day (like watching the "idiot box"—my dad's name for the TV).

6. See if you can use idiot box time to help meet your goal.

7. Turn off your cell phone. Do not be available twenty-four/seven.

Quotes on Focus

The odds of hitting your target go up dramatically when you aim at it.—Mai Pancoast

We always move in the direction of our current dominating thought.—Dennis Waitley

Shark Sense Five:
Sharks Eat to Live

Human Translation: Become a Mindful Eater

Your body doesn't need all the food you are eating. But your restless, greedy mind that craves simple pleasure and distraction wants it.—Bikram Choudhury

My husband, Pat, is unfortunately incapable of lying. A while back I asked him a stupid but all-too-common question that women ask their husbands: "Do you think I'm fat?" I remember him gently putting his hands on my shoulders, looking away for a moment, taking a long breath, and then saying the unthinkable: "Yes. But I still think you're beautiful, and I love you just the way you are." I never heard what he said after yes. I just wanted to smack him.

The truth hurts! No one wants to be fat. But being fat in our society is normal. Yes, you read that right. You are normal if you are fat, and you have a lot of company! Two-thirds of the adult population in the United States is overweight, and over one-third is obese, which means we are so fat that it puts us at risk for heart attack, cancer, stroke, and diabetes. And we just thought we looked bad.

What is interesting about sharks is that even though they are at the top of the food chain, they are not overeaters. They eat only enough food to survive. Have you ever seen a fat shark? If they are not hungry, they will swim right past you. They don't eat just because they are

bored, stressed out, or any reason other than hunger. How about us? Can we move past delicious food when we are not hungry?

I wasn't always overweight. In fact, I was one of those lucky women who could eat anything and everything and never put on weight. I assumed that I could do this for the rest of my life. After all, exercise and sports were the focal point of my life. Also, from my perspective, people who were overweight were just lazy. I didn't have any sympathy for them. My sisters were all overweight, and I figured it was because they didn't exercise. That could never happen to me!

At some point, the rules changed. I still worked out, played volleyball, and taught my fitness classes but also started to pack on the weight. It escaped my awareness because I was too busy to notice. When my clothes started to become tighter, I figured they shrank in the wash. I bought new clothes and was certain the manufacturers had made a mistake on the sizing. If I couldn't fit into my size, I wouldn't buy it. But it seemed that there were more manufacturers making mistakes. I was running out of places to shop! There also seemed to be something wrong with all the mirrors. Was it the lighting?

I also never weighed myself. What for? Nothing changed in terms of exercise or eating habits. Why then would my weight change? Then the unthinkable happened. One of my students asked me if I was pregnant. Why would she ask that? How could she say that? Was she being mean? Or was possible that I was getting …? I wouldn't even say the word.

I remember coming home with my head spinning. My husband would make me feel better. After all, he loves me no matter what. Everything will be all right, or so I thought. After my beloved husband lowered the boom, I went into the bathroom and gently stood on the scale. I almost passed out! For the first time in my life, I had to admit that I had a weight problem.

My solution was to increase the exercise. I worked out so hard that my body ached like never before. Harder, stronger, and faster were my mantras. While becoming an exercise addict, I noticed that all of my students were getting into great shape. One woman even told me that she lost twenty pounds at the end of the semester by taking just one of my aerobic classes. I taught four of those classes a day and gained five pounds. A couple of students asked how I got my new butt. They were impressed with the shape and size, but when I actually saw my butt from behind, I was in shock. Where did that come from?

Finally, it hit me. I got the wake-up call that forced me to look at my eating habits. Exercise is important, but not the most important ingredient when it comes to maintaining and losing weight, especially after a certain age. The missing link for me was nutrition. I used to be able to get away with eating anything and everything, as much as I wanted. I had become a mindless eater. Those days were over! What I needed was an eating plan that would fit into my busy lifestyle. Becoming aware of unhealthy eating habits was the first step. Skipping breakfast, grabbing junk food, driving through fast food restaurants, and eating in the car had taken their toll. Also, the portions were out of control. My body clearly did not need that much food.

We all intuitively know how to eat well—however, in today's world, it's easier said than done. We live in a society where companies spend over thirty billion dollars a year to advertise food, most of which is unhealthy. We are bombarded with misinformation, manipulation, and false claims. Most of the food we eat is high in calories, fat, and sugar, and low in nutrients and fiber. In our society, it is normal to eat foods that are unhealthy, because they are fast, convenient, and tasty.

The key is to follow our gut instincts and reconnect with our common sense. Do we need this food or do we want it? *We need to feed ourselves intentionally, rather than impulsively.* We need to plan our meals, otherwise when hunger strikes, and it will, we will succumb to vending machines and fast food restaurants that are more than happy to *feed us impulsively.*

Now, food is no longer taken for granted and it's amazing what a difference eating consciously makes in the quality of life. I know that it took years to put on the extra pounds, and they will not come off overnight, so patience is important. However, I'm busy enjoying my life and know that I am making progress. So what if I carry around a few extra pounds? I no longer need to fit into a size three pair of jeans. I am now a size eight, and I'm happy with that. Becoming a mindful eater takes some planning, but it's not hard. Plus, it makes you feel more in control in other areas of your life. It just took a while for me to see how important it is and put it into practice.

My youngest daughter, Chrissie, is a picky eater and always has been. Getting protein in her was always a challenge when she was young, since she has never liked any type of meat or vegetable. At UCLA she was once interviewed because she was one of the top athletes on campus. The interviewer was interested in her diet. How does a top athlete eat?

When I heard that she was going to be asked about her diet, I became concerned because her eating habits were anything but normal. But her answer was insightful. She said that it wasn't so much what she ate that was important. She thought the reason behind her success was that *she only ate when she was hungry and stopped when she wasn't hungry anymore.* The interviewer thought she was brilliant.

Shark Action Steps

1. Take an honest look at your eating habits.

2. Ask yourself two questions the next time you eat something:

    *   Why am I eating this?
    *   What will this do to me?

3. Don't eat while watching TV or driving. Make sure you are aware of everything you put in your mouth.

4. Eat breakfast. The energy will be used during the day, and you will feel less hungry.

5. Drink at least eight glasses of water a day. Water suppresses the appetite and helps the body metabolize stored fat.

6. When you are not eating, move your body! All exercise counts toward burning calories. Find reasons to be active!

7. When you eat a meal or a snack, do not stuff yourself. Finish your meal a little hungry instead of totally satiated.

8. Eat six small meals a day. Or eat every five hours to stabilize your metabolism.

9. Get a body composition test. This will measure how much of your body weight is fat. Over 30 percent is too high for a woman and over 25 percent is too high for a man.

10. Eat off smaller plates (nine inches is best).

11. Stay away from processed foods and fast foods. They are loaded with fat and sugar.

12. Eat lots of fresh fruits, vegetables, and whole grains.

13. Stay away from fad diets.

14. Try the 80/20 approach. Eat what you know is healthy 80 percent of the time and leave 20 percent for the not-so-nourishing foods. Most people eat improperly 80 percent of the time and healthy for only 20 percent of the time.

Quotes on Eating

Eating a vegetarian diet, walking (exercising) every day and meditating are considered radical. Allowing someone to slice your chest open and graft your leg veins to your heart is considered normal and conservative.—Dean Ornish

He that takes medicine and neglects diet wastes the skill of the physician.—Chinese proverb

Those who think they have no time for healthy eating will sooner or later have to find time for illness.—Edward Stanley

Never eat more than you can lift.—Miss Piggy

When you see the golden arches, you are probably on your way to the pearly gates.—William Castelli, MD

One should eat to live, not live to eat.—Cicero

Don't dig your grave with your own knife and fork.—English proverb

Clogged with yesterday's excess, the body drags the mind down with it.—Horace

Shark Sense Six:
Sharks Are Relentless

Human Translation: Persistence Is Its Own Reward

Many of life's failures are people who did not realize how close they were to success when they gave up.—Thomas Edison

When my older daughter, Teri, was five years old, she wanted a cat. Her school friends had cats, and she decided that she wanted one too. Since I'm allergic to cats, I explained all the reasons why we couldn't have one: "Mommy gets itchy, can't breathe, my head swells up, and I break out with sores." She looked down and walked away slowly, clearly disappointed. She returned a couple of minutes later with fire in her eyes and a new question. "Mommy, *when you die* can I have a cat?" I was in shock and said, "I guess so." She seemed happy, but I was a little scared of her after that. My daughter was not giving up easily. If it meant waiting me out, she was willing to do it. Teri was going to get her cat, one way or another.

Teri was exhibiting one of the most impressive traits of all predators, including sharks. She was relentless, persistent, and determined. Sharks never quit and neither would Teri. There is no backing down. In South Africa, white sharks will even leap out of the water to pursue their prey. Low-flying birds are not safe! Sharks will also fight to survive. They have been known to try and bite people even an hour after getting dragged from the water. They die hard!

Relentless determination is a force we can use anytime we need it. A refusal to quit on a dream is often the missing ingredient when it comes to realizing a goal. We can't just want it. We have to endure the ups and downs of any endeavor and have the confidence, self control, and the ability to stay focused on our goals. Reality forms around our commitment to success. According to John Wooden, "Success is giving 100 percent of your effort, body, mind, and soul to the struggle. That you can attain. That is success" (Wooden 1997).

There is no sudden leap to greatness. Our success lies in day-by-day actions. Good work done little by little becomes great work. Most of us give up and throw in the white towel way too soon. We expect instant results, and when our desires don't come as quickly as we want, we quit, whine, and see ourselves as victims. It's an epidemic. We have become a society of complainers who justify, rationalize, and blame others for our own shortcomings. What if you didn't know that you could quit once you decided to go after a goal? What if quitting was not an option? Would you have a better chance at being successful?

My husband's mantra is *Persistence Equals Success*. He drills this into his students and his athletes. It will be carved on his headstone when he dies. When I first encountered Pat, he was a football coach at my high school and also the study hall moderator. I never went to study hall because he wouldn't let students talk and have fun. He actually expected them to study. He was also cute, but because he was eight years older than I was and a teacher at the school, he was definitely off limits. Once he began coaching my volleyball team, I found him to be a great coach and a kind and level-headed man. I learned to trust Pat and eventually went to him to talk about boyfriend problems. He would listen to me patiently and offer good advice. As the years went on, I started to consider him not only to be my coach, but also my best friend. I could always count on him to tell it like it really was. However, I didn't feel a romantic attraction toward Pat because he was my coach, my friend, and there was that eight-year age gap. I was going after the young, stupid guys.

At some point, Pat fell in love with me. He didn't tell me because I was dating someone else at the time. On one occasion, he asked me to a party, but I thought he just wanted to give me a ride. I remember having a little too much to drink, dancing on a table, and then leaving with a new friend. Months later I found out that Pat thought it was a date. It wasn't long after the party that I broke up with my last boyfriend. That was it—I was through with men! Seeing an opportunity, Pat asked me to go to folk concert, which was a new experience for me. Pat kept asking me out, and soon we were seeing each other almost every day. I loved being with him but didn't consider him to be my boyfriend. I didn't want a boyfriend.

My parents were getting hopeful since they thought the world of Pat. I told them that nothing was going on and to back off. We were just great friends having fun. Besides, he was still my coach, and there were times at volleyball practice and during matches when I despised him. He was so picky about technique and wouldn't hesitate to tell me what I was doing wrong.

One night, he surprised me with a marriage proposal. Shocked, I looked at him in disbelief, and immediately said no. He seemed disappointed but asked me to go out again. I said sure. After all, I enjoyed being with him. I just hadn't considered marriage to him or anyone else.

A few months later he caught me off guard and proposed again. Once again, I said, "No, and don't ever ask me again." His response was interesting. He said, "I am going to ask you one more time. If you say no, I'll never see you again." That got me thinking. Was I willing to risk losing my best friend just because I was immature and didn't know anything about love? I needed time to think. For the first time in a long time, I had a reason to pray. In my heart, I knew that I loved him. Here was a great guy who knew me like no one else, faults and all, and still loved me. He was the only person in my life who didn't want me to change. We also had similar values. I had to make a choice.

Pat never asked me again. Instead, I proposed to him. Boy, did that shock everyone! Our family and friends couldn't believe that we were engaged. Some even had bets as to how long our marriage would last. After thirty years, all bets are off—our marriage is still going strong!

Like other couples, we have some rough times because we are so different from each other. He is calm, insightful, and wise, and I am outgoing, creative, and impulsive. But our differences are what keep our marriage interesting, and our similar values keep us strong. And he is still my very best friend. Pat waited eight years for me to fall in love with him. No wonder he believes persistence equals success. If he had quit on me when I first rejected him, we would not be married. He was ready for a serious relationship long before I was. He had to wait—and wait he did.

Nothing worthwhile ever comes easily, and there is no guarantee that you will achieve a particular goal even if you are persistent. However, I know that if you go after a dream relentlessly, even if you don't get what you want, the quality of your life will be better than if you didn't try at all. Persistence strengthens you. It allows doors to open that you never knew existed. If you work hard enough, you'll always get your chance to do something great. Tenacity, persistence, and perseverance are always rewarded—sometimes with outcomes better than we originally imagined. And it sure beats being a quitter.

Shark Action Steps

1. If you are going to relentlessly pursue a goal, make sure it is worth the time and effort. Ask yourself: "Do I really want this enough to put in the time and energy required to reach my goal? Is my heart in it?"

2. Ask yourself: "What am I willing to do to get the things I most want in life?"

3. To conserve energy, you must know what you can change and what you cannot. Be alert to spot a personal weakness and either correct it or use it. Don't waste your time on changing other people. That is a huge waste of energy!

4. Do not let small failures discourage you from moving toward your goal. Remember, you may have setbacks. You may even change your method, or like a shark, go under, around, over, or up. Be ready for a wild ride!

5. Anytime you feel frustration, desperation, or anger along the way, use that energy as an impetus to make alterations in your methods.

6. Visualize and sense how you will feel once you achieve your goal, and use this positive fuel to keep you going!

7. Rome was not built in a day. Give yourself time to accomplish your goal.

Quotes on Determination and Persistence

Through perseverance many people win success out of what seemed destined to be certain failure.—Benjamin Disraeli

If you believe in yourself and have the courage, the determination, the dedication, the competitive drive, and if you are willing to sacrifice the little things in life and pay the price for the things that are worthwhile, it can be done.—Vince Lombardi

People of mediocre ability sometimes achieve outstanding success because they don't know when to quit. Most men succeed because they are determined to.—George Allen

There is no chance, no destiny, no fate that can circumvent or hinder or control the firm resolve of a determined soul.—Ella Wheeler Wilcox

Any invincible determination can accomplish almost anything and in this lies the great distinction between great men and little men.—Thomas Fuller

Never grow a wishbone, daughter, where your backbone ought to be.—Clementine Paddleford

You only have to do a little more than what is asked of you to become great, because everyone else is content to just get by.—Anonymous

Shark Sense Seven:
Sharks Rely on Their Senses

Human Translation: Develop Keen Awareness

We live on the leash of our senses.—Diane Ackerman

A friend called a while back who thinks that since I am a health professor, I am also some sort of medical doctor. She wanted to discuss various symptoms she was experiencing. I suggested she call a medical expert or go to a clinic, but she wanted to talk, so I listened.

Her symptoms went like this: "I feel sick to my stomach in the morning, none of my clothes fit, my breasts are swollen and sensitive. I cry a lot for no apparent reason, have to pee all the time, and *something's moving inside.*" That should have been a big clue.

I listened patiently as she rattled off almost every pregnancy symptom known. Finally, when she paused, I asked, "Is there a possibility that you could be pregnant?" She gasped, "No! I'm still having my period." I explained to her that it is possible to be pregnant and still appear to be menstruating. My advice was to go to her doctor and have him perform a pregnancy test. I didn't trust her to do it on her own. She called me back the next day. "You were right, Sharkie, I am pregnant!" I congratulated her and asked her how far along she was. "*Six months!*" she shouted. "I only have three months to go!"

What my friend did is typical of what many of us do all the time. We focus only on what we think we know and don't look at what is happening before our very eyes. In other words, *we don't use our senses.*

Sharks have super senses and even though they are not as intelligent as humans, their senses are so attuned they depend on them for survival. Sharks feel vibrations in the water, hear sounds from miles away, and can detect one drop of blood in a million drops of water. Their keen senses are what keep them alive. Sharks have been known to migrate  for hundreds of miles, and they seem to know where they are going. Scientists believe that sharks can tune into the earth's magnetic field, allowing them to navigate over long distances. The bull shark senses salinity (salt) in the water, and its internal system can cope with dramatic changes, allowing it to swim in both the ocean and in fresh water rivers.

Even though humans don't possess the finely tuned senses of a shark, we depend on them all the time. The primary five senses of sight, smell, taste, feeling, and hearing enable us to make choices and interact with our surroundings. Staying alert and aware is just as important to our survival as it is to the shark's.

Do we have a sixth sense? Is intuition a sense we can also rely on? Many experts believe this to be the most important sense we possess. The gut feeling that is independent of cognitive reasoning is always working for us. Maybe you've caught yourself saying things like: "I had a feeling this was going to happen," or "Something inside is telling me to get out of here." Where does this sixth sense or gut feeling come from? Can we prove that it exists? How do we strengthen it? The answers are not easy; however, it's not important that we understand its source or definition. What is important is that we use its power.

A few years back, during a yoga retreat, I had the opportunity to experience a sweat lodge. The ceremony was facilitated by an authentic Native American chief. In the orientation, he explained that the sweat lodge was an ancient ritual for cleansing, spirituality, and renewal. It involved intentions, group prayer, and chanting to connect with the ancient ancestors, whom the tribe believed were preserved in the rocks on their land. I was intrigued but did not know if I could last through the hour-long ceremony because of the heat and the fact that twenty-eight people were going to participate. How were we all going to fit in that little flat tent?

We stripped down to our bathing suits. Some participants took off more, but it didn't matter because it was dark inside the sweat lodge. We crawled into the tent in single file and were not allowed to speak to one another. We sat around the rock pit in two rows with our knees up to our chests. There was no space to move in any direction. The top of the tent was three inches from our heads.

Immediately everyone started to sweat, and they hadn't even brought the hot rocks into the pit yet! Outside the tent, the "fire tender" was heating up the first batch of rocks. Every fifteen minutes, a new batch would be brought into the tent and placed in the pit. The chief said we could leave at any time if we were too uncomfortable, but if we left the ceremony, we would not be allowed back in. Hearing this set off a competitive spark in me. I promised myself: *I will not quit! I will make it through no matter what.* That was my ego talking, and it almost cost me dearly.

The ceremony began. In through the flap of the tent came the fire tender, carrying a big hook with the biggest rocks I had ever seen. He placed them in the pit. I was up in front, so I could feel the heat immediately. I broke the fastest sweat of my life in a matter of seconds. The dirt floor we were sitting on became a pool of mud within a matter of minutes. The chief started chanting, banging his drum, and moving side to side. We tried to follow without knocking anyone into the pit. At various times, the chief threw dust on the rocks, which made them spark, sizzle, and become even hotter! Every breath became a challenge. I had to breathe through my nose or it felt like fire was entering my mouth. It was becoming so hot in the tent I began to wonder how they regulated the temperature. Then I realized a scary truth: they don't!

Panic started to set in because of the claustrophobic conditions. There were so many people in the tent that the only way to move was to get up and leave. The first fifteen-minute session seemed to last forever. Finally, the flap went up and we got a breath of fresh air—just for a few seconds. Through the small opening came our friendly fire tender with more rocks—*bigger, hotter ones.* Halfway through the next segment people started to crawl out. My yoga teacher even left. At least there was more room in the tent for the stupid people like me. No matter what, I was determined to stay.

The last two segments were a blur. I had to lie on my side in the mud, which was three inches deep in sweat, to breathe. My heart was beating so fast and loud it was scary, and my chest was throbbing. Soon I realized that I was no longer sweating and the only sweat on my body was from the muddy ground. The sound of the drums and chanting was getting farther away and illuminated forms started to emerge from the rock pit and fly around the top of the lodge. Were these the ancient ancestors our chief told us about in the orientation, or was I hallucinating? A voice inside me started to scream: *Get out now!* But my legs would not move. Besides, a part of me still wanted to stay.

Finally, the flap opened for the last time. No more hot rocks. We were done! Six of us were left out of the twenty-eight that started. After inhaling the fresh cool air, I could finally sit up and breathe again. I crawled out of the tent, covered with mud from head to toe. I could barely stand up, but it felt so good to be alive! I asked my yoga teacher why she left. She told me that it was the hottest sweat lodge she had ever experienced. She was no fool.

My lungs hurt for two weeks after this experience. When my parents and husband found out about this incident, they were bewildered. How could I have been so stubborn and not gotten out of the lodge when

I had the opportunity? My mom said she heard on the news that two people died in a sweat lodge a week after my experience. They were found lying down at the end of the ceremony but could not be revived. Wow! That could have easily been me.

I learned that the ego is very strong and sometimes incredibly stupid. It's okay to be persistent and not quit, but when our senses and intuition are all giving us survival messages, we must listen! Our sweat-lodge facilitators told us that we could leave whenever we wanted. It was up to us to know whether or not we should stay. They were letting us experience an amazing ritual, and it was up to us to take care of ourselves. Unfortunately, I let my ego and stubbornness get the best of me. I might not be writing this story if I had been in the lodge five minutes longer.

Being aware of change is essential if we want to survive and improve our lives. Everyday changes occur that go unnoticed because we are not paying attention. Even our bodies constantly talk to us and tell us when something is wrong. I now call these "warning flags." But most of the time, we wait until it starts screaming in pain before we do something—which is sometimes too late.

In order to deal with a changing world, we must become more aware and learn to trust our basic instincts. Dealing with change is important in all areas of our lives. The most important part of dealing with change is to first become aware of it. And how do we do that? By using our senses.

Shark Action Steps

1. Which of the five senses are you most attuned to: vision, hearing, touch, smell, or taste?

2. When you learn something new, do you learn better when you see it, hear it, or experience it?

3. Sit quietly and take the time to experience how your body feels. Perform a body scan by working from your feet to the top of your head, or from your head down. Sense each part of your body and notice what it has to say.

4. Go into a room and notice the position of every item in the room. After a week, go into the same room and be aware of any changes. This will fine-tune your senses to notice small alterations.

5. When someone else is speaking, practice "active listening." Repeat each word to yourself immediately after the person says it. You will know if you were successful if you can relay back the information, or teach it to another.

6. On a routine walk, become aware of all the plants, sites, and beauty on your path. Be aware of the sounds, the feeling of the air. You might become aware of things that were always there, but experience them for the first time.

7. Sit quietly, and notice your thoughts. Imagine your thoughts are clouds moving along the sky. Observe them from a distance, and let them pass. Do not feel anything or question their existence.

8. Learn to notice how your body feels when you are upset or angry. Does your stomach, throat, or head hurt? This is a mind-body response we all need to be aware of, as a negative mind can and usually does interfere with the normal functioning of the body. It's as if your body's cells are eavesdropping in on your thoughts.

Learn to listen to your body, and take care of it when you are feeling stressed.

Quotes on Senses and Awareness

When you start using senses you've neglected, your reward is to see the world with completely fresh eyes.—Barbara Sher

The moment one gives close attention to anything, even a blade of grass, it becomes a mysterious, awesome, indescribable, magnificent world in itself.—Henry Miller

Let us not look back in anger or forward in fear, but around in awareness.—James Thurber

Shark Sense Eight:
Sharks Are Fearless

Human Translation: Growth Happens When We Are the Most Uncomfortable

I must not fear. Fear is the mind-killer. Fear is the little-death that brings total obliteration. I will face my fear. I will permit it to pass over me and through me. And when it has gone past, I will turn the inner eye to see its path. Where the fear has gone, there will be nothing. Only I will remain.—Frank Herbert

It was a cold winter day in Sun Valley, Idaho, the ultimate destination for serious skiers. I was skiing alone, enjoying the mountain, when a man stopped me at the bottom of a run. He was all decked out in a classy ski outfit and had brand-new, top-of-the-line skis. My skis were banged up, and my parka was tattered because I wore it every day. The man asked me if I wanted a new pair of skis and a parka for free! I thought he was kidding. "Sure!" I said quickly. What do I have to do?"

He explained that all I had to do was ski as fast as I could down Exhibition Run. My heart stopped for a minute. Did he really say *Exhibition*? That was the toughest run on the mountain. It was full of moguls and had a fall line that was not only steep, but also crooked. There was a chairlift above it, so the people on the chair could either see how great you were skiing, or watch you struggle or fall all the way to the bottom. My first impulse was to say "No way!" but I really wanted the new skis and parka, so instead I said, "Okay."

It started to snow lightly as we took the chairlift to the top of the run. I noticed there were several television cameras because a dual slalom race was going on. Exhibition had been sectioned off for the event and no one could ski on the run except for the competitors. I looked at my new acquaintance and asked, "Do you expect me to race?"

"Yes" he replied with a slight grin on his face. "One of our competitors had to pull out of the race, and I had to find someone fast. You are her replacement. Everything has been taken care of." Fear gripped me. What had I gotten myself into? Was I absolutely nuts? A part of me wanted to jump off of the chairlift. Instead, I acted like I was confident and tried to hide my shaking knees. When I got off the chairlift, I received my new skis, a jacket, and a racing bib with a number on it. The man also gave me new goggles and a hat, and then told me to wait my turn. My heart started to race, my legs were shaking, and I was taking two breaths a second. I was scared! Several of the skiers were speaking in foreign languages. Was this an international race?

Over the loudspeaker, the announcer introduced a female skier. She was one of my all-time idols. The next name he called was also another of my favorite skiers. Her name was Sue. I couldn't wait to see these two great athletes race against each other. My new friend turned to me and said, "Sharkie, you're up!"

I gasped. "What do you mean I'm up?"

He gave me a devious look and said, "You're taking Sue's spot."

Before I could resist, he dragged me over to the starting gate. I was in shock. Could he actually get away with this? It was snowing lightly, so you couldn't really tell that I was not this awesome skier. I had the same build, the same skis, hat, goggles, jacket, and bib that she would have worn had she been there. At the starting gate the other competitor said, "Hi Suzy!" I gave her a weak smile and nodded. I felt like such an imposter.

The gun went off! I was hoping that it would have shot me at that point, but I was off. The big race was on! To my surprise, I got through the first half of the race without trouble. I was neck to neck with my opponent—skiing like a champion until ….

Suddenly, without warning, I caught an edge and flipped over sideways. You could hear the crowd's dismay as I crashed and burned and hurtled down the rest of the run on my backside. All the cameras were on me. When I came to a stop, instead of going to the bottom of the run, I broke through a side barrier and started to ski off through the forest. I knew that no one would follow me since that area was marked "off limits." I can only imagine what was said on the broadcast about Sue's skiing that day.

I never saw my new "friend" again, but I kept all the new equipment, conquered my fear, and was rewarded for my effort. After all, I did ski as fast as I could all the way to the bottom. I just took a different route! If I hadn't tried, I would have skied the rest of the season in that old parka and battered skis.

The word *fear* elicits all sorts of negative feelings and messages. We don't want fear in our lives! But without fear, what would we ever accomplish? The key is not to avoid fear, but to move through it and utilize its power. We have all experienced fear on occasion, and sometimes it can be our best teacher. How we respond to uncertainty is what makes us different from one another. We can choose to let fear cripple us, or we can move through it and experience all that it has to offer. If we can control fear, it can make us stronger for the task at hand.

Top athletes and performers are masters at getting fired up for the main event. The upset stomach, the jitters, and sweating are symptoms that their bodies and minds are getting ready to perform at the highest level. The energy that fear provides allows us to be stronger, move faster, and perform better. And it helps knowing that there is a reward at the end!

One of my best athletes started to get nervous before the National Championship Volleyball finals. Her stomach was churning, and she was flushed and shaking. She told me that she didn't think she could play because she felt sick. Realizing that she was scared and not sick, I told her that her symptoms were caused by her body getting ready to play the best volleyball in her life. Luckily for me, she believed me and went out on the court and played awesome.

Sharks use fear to their advantage. They don't back down from a challenge because they are afraid. Instead, they use the energy fear provides and act with even more intensity. They accept fear  as a fact of life that is necessary for their survival. They are not afraid of negative outcomes. If they are not successful, they simply move on to the next challenge without embarrassment or hard feelings.

Staying with routines is always easier than exploring the unknown. Living in a comfort zone keeps us stuck and can suck the life out of us. No one who changes the world plays it safe. We must be willing to experience fear in order to change our lives for the better. Our new lives are waiting on the other side. Moving in a new direction is stimulating! John Wooden states: "The man who is afraid to risk failure seldom has to face success." How true. No one ever accomplished anything of value without risking failure. In fact, some of our most famous achievers were huge "failures" before they became successful.

Fears we imagine are usually worse than what may actually exist. Sometimes we even make up things to be afraid of or make mountains out of molehills. We play the game "what if" and visualize negative outcomes for moving outside of our cushy, comfortable abyss of apathy. We need to change our focus on what we want, instead of what, if anything, we will lose. Seeing change as a challenge is a powerful impetus that helps us utilize the power of fear. If we want to be successful, we have to want more than comfort and must move into uncertainty and risk failure in order to succeed.

From a shark point of view, *the tastiest food is always in uncharted waters.*

Shark Action Steps

1. Ask yourself: "What would I do if I were not afraid?"

2. Pick one goal or task that you want to do but keep putting off because fear gets in the way.

3. Schedule this task in the next two weeks.

4. Find out as much as you can about it so you are prepared.

5. Look for people who will help and support you, not fuel your fears.

6. Picture yourself being successful at completing the task.

7. Persist until you are successful.

8. Notice the new sense of empowerment and accomplishment you experience from overcoming this fear.

Quotes on Fear and Failure

For every fear I have had, ninety-nine percent have been groundless once action was taken.—Bryon Pulsifer

Most people achieved their greatest success one step beyond what looked like their greatest failure.—Brian Tracy

Failure will never overtake me if my determination to succeed is strong enough.—Og Mandino

I've come to believe that all my past failure and frustration were actually laying the foundations for the understanding that has created the new level of living I now enjoy.—Tony Robbins

Forget about the consequences of failure. Failure is only a temporary change in direction to set you straight for your next success.
—Dennis Waitley

What you fear is that which requires action to overcome.
—Byron Pulsifer

Fear of failure is one attitude that will keep you at the same point in your life.—Byron Pulsifer

Shark Sense Nine:
Sharks Are Flexible

Human Translation: Adapt and Thrive

The way I see it, if you want the rainbow, you gotta put up with the rain.
—Dolly Parton

Success is never a straight path. There are always detours, roadblocks, and obstacles in the way. Being able to deal with these curveballs is what makes our lives challenging, exciting, and productive. How many people do you know who don't adapt well to setbacks? They are the complainers who quit when they don't get what they want or when things don't go exactly as planned. Who knows? Something much bigger and better might have been just around the corner if they were more flexible and open to possibilities instead of being rigid and expecting life to follow their exact plans.

Unless we are willing to be flexible and go with the flow of life, we get left behind. The reason we don't feel comfortable with change relates back to fear—we're afraid of the unknown. Not only do we need to handle fear, but we must be willing to explore a new direction if something does not work out as planned. Having expectations is okay, as long as we *don't get attached to the outcome.* The twists and turns and ups and downs are what make life interesting. Would you really want to be able to predict every single event in your life? Where's the joy in that?

Sharks are flexible not only because their skeletons are made of cartilage, but because they do not have expectations. Even though they are one of the fiercest predators on the planet, they are also adaptable. They can change when life changes. They are able to adapt to change because they are always in the present

moment. Past and future events do not hold any power over them. They respond to the challenges in the moment. The "one that got away" is not a setback to them. They just keep going, swimming around any obstacles, and are ready for action at all times.

Having children was not on my agenda. My life would be fine and fulfilling without them—or so I thought. Also, I didn't think I could be a good mother because I never played with dolls or enjoyed babysitting. It just wasn't for me. My sister was the one who wanted to have kids. She got married at nineteen and started having children right away. When our family would get together, her four kids would be running around, yelling, screaming, and causing all kinds of commotion. They were adorable and fun, but they moved like four small tornados going in different directions. At times, she looked overwhelmed.

I tried to give her some little sister advice and suggested that she attend parenting classes. I thought I was qualified since I minored in psychology at UCLA and was studying childhood behavior. Besides, I also loved getting the upper hand when she was vulnerable, since I didn't have many opportunities when I was young. She rolled her eyes and said to me, "If you think it's so easy, why don't you have kids?" I told her that I would when it was time (yeah, right) and added that I would be great at it since I was *so educated*. She was not amused.

Life handed me a surprise when I became pregnant with my first child. My sister was more excited than I was and could not wait for me to have this baby. Not only did she want to be an aunt, but I think she also wanted me to eat my words about how easy it was to be a mom. I knew a lot about child psychology, but absolutely nothing about babies. I was in trouble. However, I decided to go for it and do the best I could.

As the pregnancy progressed, my husband and I prepared to have our baby naturally, without any drugs. I figured that it was the best way to give the baby a great start and felt confident that I could handle the labor. We practiced our breathing patterns religiously and were fired up for the big event. I even told Pat, "No matter what happens in the labor room, don't let them give me drugs." He promised he would honor my wishes. I had a real coach to help me through labor. I was confident we could get through anything. I was ready—or so I thought.

Finally, the day came. I expected to breeze through the labor and push the baby out with one try since I had trained very hard for this event. In fact, I even told my doctor that when it was time to push he'd better be ready because this baby was going to hit the wall.

The first two hours went smoothly—the breathing patterns worked and we seemed like a perfect team. I kept thinking, *This isn't so bad.* But the last hour was a different story. It felt like a cement truck had rolled onto my stomach and wouldn't get off. It just kept moving back and forth. My contractions were coming so fast and hard that I barely knew when one started and the other one stopped. I started to doubt my abilities. The sweet nurses would drop in periodically and ask me if I wanted anything for the pain. Before I could open my mouth, Pat would say: "No, she's doing fine."

Fine? You must be kidding, I thought. Finally, I started to beg Pat to allow the nurses to give me something for the pain. "*Puleeze,* Packy. I'll do anything." I'll never forget what happened next. He picked me up by my hospital gown, shook me, and yelled, "Dammit, compete!" The nurses and doctors were in shock. It was like he was coaching me at an athletic event. No drugs for me!

Somehow, I got to the point where the doctor finally said I could push. I was ready—or so I thought. I pushed as hard as I could. "Where is it?" I asked, fully expecting to see the baby. "Push again, again … again … again …." I was not expecting this! I even passed out once, and no one noticed. When I woke up, they just kept saying, "Push, again … again …." Finally a cry rang out in the room that did not come from me. It was my baby! Instantly, I was a mother! When they put Teri into my arms, I immediately fell in love. All the pushing and pain was worth it. She sucked her hand and looked at me curiously, as if she was sizing me up.

I had heard all the horror stories of sleepless nights and crying babies, but Teri was different. She was good-natured, hardly ever cried, and when I put her down, she would coo. She even slept through the night. It was like having an animated doll. Everyone was amazed at what a good baby she was and what a great mother I turned out to be! Everyone, that is, except for my sister, Moe. She was not buying it. "Why don't you have another one?" she suggested slyly. I replied, "Sure! I could have ten of these!"

My second daughter, Chrissie, came along four years later. I was excited for Teri to have a sister or brother. She was already handling her dolls better than I handled her. She could help me. But this pregnancy was different. I was fatigued and sick during the whole nine months. However, I was ready to do a better job in the labor room, since I almost bailed out last time. I also convinced Pat that maybe some of the drugs weren't so bad. I was ready for anything, except an emergency Cesarean delivery. Chrissie was breach and could not be turned around. They had to get her out fast. It's a good thing they did, because her umbilical cord was hooked up to the amniotic sac instead of the placenta. She would not have survived a normal birth.

Chrissie was definitely a different baby than Teri from the get-go. I was expecting another animated doll, but it was not to be. I remember the first time our eyes met. She let out the loudest scream I ever heard. I knew I wasn't in Kansas anymore! This poor baby was colicky, didn't like to be breast-fed, and did not sleep through the night for the first two years! Chrissie was full of surprises. For example, she never really crawled. Instead, at six months old, she pulled herself up and started to run! I certainly wasn't expecting that. Thank goodness I had Teri and Pat to help since she was a whirling dervish. Now I had my own little tornado but felt extremely lucky to have the opportunity to experience the storm.

Our family has had a lifetime of amazing memories and experiences. As I look back, I can barely remember being married without the kids. And to think I didn't want them originally. Now I can't imagine my life without them. Teri recently got married, and Chrissie was her maid of honor—they were both so beautiful and happy. I still can't believe what a gift they are and how proud I am to be their mom. Going with the flow of life is so much more fulfilling than being an obsessive control freak. Being a parent is profound, important, and wonderful. It challenges you to balance work and life changes and also see the world through different eyes—your kids'. I realize it's not for everyone, but for me, it was life changing and well worth the effort.

Do you remember singing the following song when you were a child? *Row, row, row your boat/Gently down the stream/Merrily, merrily, merrily, merrily/Life is but a dream.* This simple song has an important message for all of us. It appears that many of us are paddling against the current and always unhappy when we can't get what we want immediately or get something that we didn't ask for. Why not try to lighten up a bit and see where the current takes you? It might move you into different territory, but there will be a lot of scenery and memories along the way, and you just might end up better off than if you continually fight against the stream of life. Sharks don't swim against the current, and they usually end up getting exactly what they want.

There is a famous prayer entitled the "The Serenity Prayer." I often read it to my yoga students and we then discuss how to apply this passage into our daily lives:

God grant me the serenity
to accept the things I cannot change;
the courage to change the things I can;
and the wisdom to know the difference.

My students often share that they do spend too much time trying to change the things that they cannot—like the past, or other people—and don't spend enough time trying to change the things they can—like themselves. By shifting awareness and being more flexible in our lives, we open the doors for greater opportunities to present themselves.

Shark Action Steps

1. In what part of your life are you set in your ways?

2. What are you missing out on because of your near-sightedness?

3. If you always have the same meal at a restaurant, be adventurous and ask for the special of the day. Order it and eat it! (I only got sick once doing this.)

4. When someone says no to you, ask for the same thing in a different way.

5. Learn to communicate using both verbal and nonverbal language. Learn from responses what works and what doesn't work with people.

6. Don't expect other people and situations to change to suit you. Be willing to look at things from a different perspective. Be willing to walk in another person's shoes.

7. To conserve energy, know what you can change and what you cannot. The only person you can change is you! And the most basic thing you can change is your attitude.

The following passage is excerpted from the sermon *Strengthening Your Grip on Attitudes* (SYG7A) by Charles Swindoll.[2] The complete sermon can be heard online at www.insight.org.

Attitudes

"The longer I live, the more I realize the impact of attitude on life.

Attitude to me is more important than the facts.

It is more important than the past,

Than education, than money,

Than circumstances, than failures, than successes,

It is more important than appearance, giftedness, or skill.

It will make or break a company.

It will cause a church to soar or sink.

It will be the difference in a happy home or a home of horror.

The remarkable thing is you have a choice every day regarding the attitude you will embrace for that day.

We cannot change our past.

We cannot change the fact that people will act in a certain way.

We cannot change the inevitable.

The only thing we can do is play on the one thing we have, and that is our attitude.

I am convinced that life is ten percent what happens to me and ninety percent how I react to it.

And so it is with you."

Shark Sense Ten:
Sharks Sleep with Their Eyes Open

Human Translation: Be on the Lookout! Opportunities Are Everywhere

When one door closes, another opens. But we often look so regretfully upon the closed door that we don't see the one that has opened for us.
—Helen Keller

When I heard that sharks sleep with their eyes open, I was intrigued but also skeptical. How can any creature do that? I had to see for myself, so I went to the Aquarium of the Pacific in Long Beach, California, and visited the famous shark lagoon.

I peered through the glass as the sharks moved slowly across the pool at eye level. They glided past me, gazing out of the sides of their yellowish-white eyeballs with cold, ghostly stares. Small kids were screaming and jumping up and down every time one of these hulky creatures swam toward the viewing window. Some of the parents were screaming too. The sharks ignored their "fans" and were clearly not amused.

Finally, I noticed a large black motionless figure at the bottom of the tank about four feet from the window. At first I thought this shark might be sick or dead, since all the other sharks were moving, but I was close enough to see his eyes. He was definitely not dead. The shark was still, but his eyes were wide open. As a fish swam by, his eyes followed it. When he was not watching the other fish swim, he was watching us. His body was motionless; however, his eyes were very much alive. The gaze felt eerie, and for some reason I could not stop looking at this strange shark. All of the sudden, a small fish swam directly in front of our viewing path. The shark narrowed his eyes and suddenly sprang into action. The movement was so powerful and fast that it was shocking, especially since he was virtually motionless before that moment. Just because a shark isn't moving doesn't mean that he's not alert. He is always ready for action.

I'm not suggesting that we should sleep with our eyes open; however, we need to be alert and on the lookout at all times for opportunities to grow and spice up our lives. Setbacks are often discouraging, such as losing a job or a relationship. However, they often become the stage for future success and serve to block a path that would probably not lead to achieving lifelong goals. Have you ever broken up with a partner and thought that you would never again find love? Trust me—there are plenty of fish in the sea who are also looking. Get out there and start fishing, or better yet, start swimming!

I was fired once and traumatized for a while because I thought I would never find another job as great as the one I had lost. Clothes and shoes were almost as important as volleyball, so when I landed a sales position at a popular shoe store, in my mind, I had died and gone to heaven! There was a Fashion Circle in the middle of the store where we sold clothes, and I even got an employee discount. Even though this was just a part-time job to help out with school, I figured that it didn't get any better than this.

One day, a woman came into the store looking for jeans and found a couple of styles she wanted to try on. I took her items to our makeshift dressing area, which consisted of a sheet tacked to the ceiling draped part way to the floor. If you were trying something on, everyone in the store could see you from the knees down. I noticed that she had selected all size eights, which was clearly *not* her size. I politely told her that the jeans ran small, but she glared at me and said they were fine. I waited patiently outside while she squeezed herself into the first pair. Strange groaning noises were coming from the dressing room, and people started to watch as the curtains were shaking.

Finally, she parted the sheet to look at herself in the mirror. She had clearly performed a miracle by getting the pants on, but now the zipper was stuck. I could actually see a portion of the side seam starting to burst! "How do they look?" she asked. I said I thought they were a tad small, and I would be happy to fetch another size. She frowned and returned to the dressing area and proceeded to try to remove the pants. More noises. Finally, I heard a soft voice say, "Miss, oh miss! Can you help me?" As I opened the sheet, I noticed there was a huge cockroach stuck in the zipper of the jeans. Its legs were moving a hundred miles an hour in a futile effort to escape being crushed. The look on my face said it all. I was horrified!

The woman looked down at the zipper, noticed the bulging squirmy body, and started to scream! "Help! Help! Get me out of these pants, *now!*" I pulled, tugged, and strained. Nothing worked! Finally, I told the woman to lie down on the ground. I grabbed the bottoms of the pant legs and pulled as hard as I could while she kicked her legs almost as fast as the poor cockroach! The store was full of customers at the time. You would think that someone would have come to our aid, but instead they all watched to see a screaming woman being dragged across the floor in the dressing area.

Finally, the jeans came off! Instead of thanking me for rescuing her, the woman grabbed her belongings and ran out of the store in her *underpants*! My manager was furious with me for dragging a customer across the floor and would not believe my story. I could not find any evidence of the cockroach, which was probably smashed to smithereens, and was immediately fired from my dream job.

What now? I certainly couldn't ask for a reference! Who would hire a girl named after a shark who supposedly had assaulted a woman in a shoe store dressing room? I was nineteen years old and thought my career was over. Yes, my career as a shoe salesperson was over, but I had other options. I continued my education and ultimately landed a full-time job as a volleyball coach and a professor—a job that I still enjoy today.

Things happen for reasons we are not always aware of. We usually don't have the ability to gaze into our futures and see what's ahead. Sometimes, losing a favorite job or ending a relationship is what is necessary to get us going in another direction. Humans usually are motivated by either inspiration or desperation. The positive route is more pleasant, but desperation is usually much more of an impetus for change. Radical life changes teach us resiliency and usually put us on a new path. I know I might have sold shoes for a much longer time if I hadn't gotten fired. It forced me to look in another direction right away and find a better job, which ultimately lead to a better life and a career I'm actually good at. Being forced into a new situation is sometimes necessary to grow.

My daughter Teri came to me when she was nine years old holding two Easter baskets filled with eggs and toys two days before Easter. She had found the goodies in my closet and had some questions for me. She narrowed her eyes and asked me flat out: "Is there an Easter Bunny?" I sighed and waited to make sure I wanted to tell her the truth. Then I blurted out: "Yes, I'm the Easter Bunny. Every Easter I get the baskets and fill them up with goodies for you and your sister." She looked at me strangely, and then shook her head as if she suspected it all along. But she wanted to know more. "Are you also the Tooth Fairy?"

My daughter was starting to put things together. "Yes," I replied. "I was pretty lousy at that job, huh?" She started to giggle and said she agreed since many times I would forget to put the money under the pillow and take the tooth. "Are you Santa Claus too?" she asked. I admitted my role as the jolly old man and told her that it was really hard the year she wanted a special doll and all the stores were sold out. Desperate, I bought an imposter doll that cost over eighty dollars. We both started to laugh hysterically. She remembered how much she hated that doll because it wasn't the one she wanted.

Finally, she looked at me in horror with even bigger eyes. Her voice was shaking. "Are you Jesus?" she asked. "No!" I gasped. "I can't take credit for that."

My daughter changed that day and made a transition to becoming more grown-up. She was ready to move on. We all go through stages when we are challenged to look at life differently. These transitions are necessary for us to grow. In every stage we can either focus on the negative side or look for the opportunities and possibilities they present.

Shark Action Steps

1. Look back at an event where you were forced to make a radical change.

2. Were you confused as to why this event or situation happened to you?

3. Did you do anything to deserve this outcome?

4. Since that time, what has changed in your life for the better?

5. Would these positive changes have taken place if you did not have the negative experience first?

6. Instead of regarding the event as negative, view it instead as a turning point that moved you forward to a new path.

The following is an inspirational passage from Donald Hurzeler, a successful business man and writer. As a cancer survivor, he is a master of teaching people not only how to be successful in business and life, but also how to rebound from life's unpleasant beatings. His new book, *The Way Up: How to Keep Your Career Moving in the Right Direction*, is required reading for anyone who wants to maximize their career potential.

A Winner in Waiting

Are you beaten down by life
Have you lost another race
Were you second at the finish
Has life slapped you in the face?

Is the world around you saying
That you're just not good enough
That someone does it better
That you just don't have the stuff?

I've got news for you my buddy
Let me tell you what I know
I'm aware of all your talents
This defeat is but a blow.

So get up off the canvas
Don't be jealous, don't be mad
Focus once again on winning
Victory's out there to be had.

The loss comes only
When you give up the fight
When you agree to be a loser
When you finally say "They're right."

You are a winner now in waiting
First prize will come, my friend
Work hard and you will get it
The only question's "When?"

Don't let others tell you different
They don't know you like I do
You're a winner, don't forget it
The next champion will be you!

Used with permission from Donald J. Hurzeler, *Designated for Success*, 157-158

Shark Sense Eleven:
Sharks Have Thick Skin

Human Translation: Toughen Up

You are beaten to earth? Well, well, what's that? Come up with a smiling face. It's nothing against you to fall down flat, but to lie there—that's disgrace.—Edmund Vance Cooke

Don't you hate being around people who complain and whine all of the time? I know I do. You become afraid to say anything to these pathetic souls or even look a certain way because it might hurt their feelings and give them something else to complain about. It feels as if they are sucking the life force right out of you.

Guess what? They are. Notice how you feel when these people approach you, unload their woes, and then leave. They feel better; you feel worse. Is this any way to live? Is that what we want to share?

I have a friend who is amazingly funny, spontaneous, and loyal. The problem is that there is a big price to pay for these perks, and sometimes when I see her coming, I look for cover. A good deal of time and energy is often spent on empathizing with her many woes. I try to be nice and give advice, but the other day I couldn't help but scream, "Get over it!" She is now avoiding me. But I feel better.

Have you ever noticed that people who complain seem to find more and more to complain about? It's as though they have a cloud following them around that dumps slime on them. This is no accident. There is a universal law that says: *What you think about expands.* If a person is focused on the negative, guess what? He or she gets more of the same. Instead of focusing of what we don't have, we should focus on what we do have and be thankful. Then maybe we will get more good stuff!

Consider the following story:

An employer called in two of his workers who held the same position for a conference. He wanted to know how they were doing and if there were any concerns. The first worker complained about everything and everybody and said that he couldn't stand the job and wished that everyone would shape up to his standards. The boss sat and smiled but was thinking: *If you think this is bad, just wait and see. It can get much worse.* The next week, the employee was demoted and had to do more work with less pay.

When the second employee was asked how he was doing, he said that he was happy to have his job and felt challenged, but was enjoying the ride. He was upbeat, positive, and eager to make things better if given the chance. The boss sat there, smiled, and thought to himself: *If you think this is good, just wait. It can be even better!* The worker was promoted, got a raise, and became a partner in the business.

Shifting awareness can be very powerful. The above story illustrates that while both employees had the same job, one chose to focus on the negative while the other focused on the positive. We have the ability to make this shift at any time, for any life situation.

Sharks have thick skin and are resilient to matters that are insignificant. They don't focus on what is wrong and move effort- lessly toward their goals. They save their energy and  strength for the important matters. A shark doesn't take anything person- ally. Even if they are wounded, they go about their business. They don't sulk or find other sharks to commiserate with. If they are hurt or sick, they do what it takes to survive.

I once had an amazing friend by the name of Diana. Our daughters were on a gymnastics team together and we used to sit in the stands and feel each other's pain and excitement as our daughters flew around bars, did back flips on the balance beam, and hurled their bodies over a vault. We shared a lot of joy, excitement, and sheer terror.

A while back, Diana was diagnosed with breast cancer. She had surgery, did chemo, and went back to her job teaching and raising her five beautiful children. She was too busy for cancer to ruin her life.

But it came back for a second round. This time it spread to her bones and she was diagnosed with stage four cancer. Diana made a decision that she was not going to give up. She went on chemo again, lost her beautiful hair in one week, and endured fatigue and nausea—the common side effects of the treatment. She bought a stylish wig to cover up her bald head and continued to work full time, focusing on her first grade students. She didn't let anyone know about her illness except her family and best friends. She didn't want sympathy—what she wanted was to continue to make a difference and enjoy whatever time she had left.

She also decided that it was time to do some serious traveling. Diana and her husband became a cruise couple and traveled all around the world. We were lucky enough to go with them to the Caribbean and had so much fun it was hard to believe that my friend was so sick. We lived like there was no tomorrow. We spent every day at the spa being pampered with exotic treatments, danced every night, drank the most expensive wine, went on all the excursions, and gambled to our heart's content. I spent so much money that I am still paying for it, but it was worth every penny.

Diana never complained about her condition. Instead, she used it as a reason to enjoy life to the fullest. None of her colleagues or students knew that she was battling cancer. When she listened to their problems, she would just smile and offer advice. If they only knew the truth, I'm sure they would have felt silly about telling her their trivial problems. My friend found the upside of being diagnosed with a deadly disease. Instead of closing her eyes and feeling sorry for herself, she opened up, embraced life, and found a new purpose in being an incredible example for her friends and family. She fought her cancer with dignity and grace and left an incredible legacy when she finally passed away.

Shortly after her passing, one of my students came up to me after class and started playing the whining game—complaining about school, her family, her health, and anything else that she thought would get a sympathetic ear. She was a mess! I finally said, "If you stop complaining about your life, maybe it will get better." She looked at me as if I had just landed from Mars. However, she didn't use me as a dumping ground anymore for her problems, and I think she might have toughened up a little—at least when she was around me.

In case no has told you—life is tough. It's supposed to be. The measure of us as people is not the kinds of problems or challenges we have—it's how we handle them. When we get knocked down, do we stay there or get back up? If you saw the *Rocky* movies, you know that this was the major theme and one reason why Balboa became such a hit—he was always getting knocked down but he never stayed down, much to his opponents' surprise.

So what's it going to be? Are you going to toughen up and handle life's challenges and be thankful for what you have or lie there and moan and be a victim? It's your choice.

Shark Action Steps

1. Are there times when you have dumped your life on others just to get attention?

2. Is that the kind of attention you want? To have others see you as a victim?

3. Do these people now try to avoid you or do they reciprocate by dumping problems on you and trying to get one up on being a bigger, better victim?

4. Is this an empowering relationship?

5. What can you do if you're involved in this type of negative symbiotic relationship?

6. Focus on what you have in your life that is positive and give thanks.

7. If you can't think of anything, go to an area of town where there are homeless people, or go to a hospital and visit the burn unit, or to a shelter, and see what real problems look like.

8. The best therapy for a person who feels sorry for himself or herself is to help another human being.

9. There is no prize for being the best victim or the best martyr. Life rewards those who help themselves.

Quotes on Toughening Up

Don't complain about the problem—fix it!—Hank Med

Look for the good and you will find it. Look for the bad and you will find that too.—Author unknown

Shark Sense Twelve:
Sharks Do Not Experience Self-Doubt

Human Translation: Confidence Opens Doors

Men are born to succeed, not fail.—Henry David Thoreau

F ull-time faculty jobs at the college don't open up very often, and when they do, we have a lot of applicants and the competition is fierce. A while back I was asked to serve on the hiring committee for a new position in our department. We had several qualified applicants, but one stood out from the rest—at least on paper. She had twice as many references and educational achievements than any of the others. Since she was in my area of expertise, I was excited to meet her.

When she came into the room, I'll never forget my first impression. I thought: *Is this the right woman?* Her posture was slouched, she had her head down, and her clothes were wrinkled. It almost looked like she rolled out of bed and came to the interview. She smiled weakly at us, sat down, and then reached into her purse for some note cards. I decided to forego my first impression and focus on her resume, but when she spoke, I became even more concerned. Her voice was shaky and soft, she answered the questions hesitantly, without conviction, and kept looking at her cards for what she thought would be the perfect answer. Needless to say, she made a very poor first impression. Even though she seemed sweet and intelligent, as she was talking I was imagining how she would function teaching our classes. I knew the students would eat her up.

We almost did not interview our next applicant because her application was messy, and she only had two references instead of three. But when she walked into the room, we took notice. She was dressed in a classy navy blue suit and marched into the room with an air of confidence. She was perfectly groomed and was beaming with excitement! I'll never forget her smile. She looked us all right in the eyes and said: "Who wants to ask me the first question?" Even though her answers were not the typical responses we usually receive from job applicants, she was so confident and strong in her delivery that we didn't even consider disagreeing with her! Who do you think got the job?

There's no such thing as a timid or an arrogant shark. Sharks do not experience self-doubt and do not try to impress, but always command respect. Sharks are confident and move toward their goals unobstructed by insecurity. When humans go after goals, some of us are either at the timid end of the self-esteem spectrum or at the arrogant end. Sharks are right smack dab in the middle—right where we should be.

We all experience self-doubt at times, and it is normal to feel uncomfortable in a new situation. But if we are going after something important, we must not allow self-doubt to creep into our consciousness. Sometimes, we even have to fake confidence in order to succeed. A strong first impression has a lasting effect! Most people make up their minds about you in the first few seconds. You want those seconds to be your best if you are going after something important. There is no room for self-doubt. Save that for your therapist.

At the other end of the spectrum are people who appear too confident and arrogant. We had another applicant we interviewed who could not stop bragging about all his accomplishments. We even had to ask that he shorten his comments a couple of times because of time constraints, so we could ask all the questions required in the interview. He used each question as an opportunity to try and impress us and didn't even answer the question. Needless to say—we were not impressed. People who exhibit this type of behavior seem to be self-assured, but usually are anything but confident. The truth is, they have poor self-esteem. These are your arrogant showboats who are always bragging and trying to get attention. It's almost as if they're saying: "Watch me, Mama! Watch me!"

You know the type. They love to talk. A conversation usually goes like this: "*I* blah, blah, blah, *and I did* blah, blah, blah, *and I have the best* blah, blah, blah, *and I just bought* blah, blah, blah, *and maybe you should* blah, blah, blah *because I now can* blah, blah, blah." The two words these people say the most are *and* (so you can't get a word in) and *I.* The effect this person has on you is similar to a flying insect that keeps buzzing around your head. You just wish you had a huge fly swatter! What's amazing is that these people never want to know how your life is going. If you should happen to get in a word, they will interject the minute you take a breath and make you feel like what you just said is unimportant compared to what they have to say next.

Some of the most confident people I know don't talk much. They don't have to. Their actions speak louder than words, and they are great listeners. Leaders have confidence in their abilities, good communication skills, are level-headed, and can retain a good perspective.

When a shark swims into an area, it doesn't have to show its teeth or attack in order to get noticed, and neither do we. Confidence comes from knowing that whatever happens, we will be okay. We don't need other people to make us feel good. Self-esteem has nothing to do with other people looking up to you or showing respect. That is neediness. We can always find that respect and love within ourselves.

Shark Action Steps

1. Replace the words "I can't" with "I won't."

2. Replace the words "I have to" with "I choose to."

3. Take good care of your body. Confidence comes from feeling comfortable in your own body.

4. Remember, you cannot truly impress others if you do not have confidence in yourself.

5. True confidence comes from overcoming challenges in life. Instead of avoiding change, go after it!

Confidence Quotes

Nobody can make you feel inferior without your consent.
—Eleanor Roosevelt

If there is no enemy on the inside, the one on the outside cannot hurt you.—African proverb

It's not who you are that holds you back, it's who you think you are not.—Author unknown

Whether you think you can or think you can't, you are right.
—Henry Ford

If you put a small value on yourself, rest assured, the world will not raise your price.—Author unknown

Confidence comes not from always being right, but from not fearing to be wrong.—Peter T. McIntyre

Aerodynamically the bumble bee shouldn't be able to fly; but the bumble bee doesn't know it so it goes on flying anyway.
—Mary Kay Ash

What lies behind us and what lies before us are tiny matters compared to what lies within us.—Ralph Waldo Emerson

Shark Sense Thirteen:
Sharks Fend for Themselves

Human Translation:
Get Away from the Maddening Crowd

No one can possibly achieve any real and lasting success or 'get rich' in business by being a conformist.—J.P. Getty

Once upon a time in a land far away, a colony of frogs had a race to see who could climb the highest peak the fastest. Only the bravest tried, while the rest watched and cheered them on. The competition began and the crowd was cheering wildly from below. A few of the frogs started to approach the top of the steep peak. The crowd, sensing danger, started shouting, "Oh no! You'll never make it! The peak is too high! Come down before you get hurt!"

Hearing this, the frogs started to descend the peak, all except for one. He kept climbing until he made it all the way to the top. He was the hero! The crowd let out a thunderous roar. When this brave frog came down to get his prize, he was asked how he made it to the top, but he did not respond. Finally, one of the frogs recognized that it was Henry, who happened to be different from the others because he was hearing-impaired. Henry could not hear the crowd telling him to come down, and therefore was the only one that succeeded!

As long as we are alive, we will always have society telling us what we can and cannot do. The media is especially powerful in influencing us and our decisions about how we should be living our lives. Critics are everywhere and getting stronger every day. We even pay them for their discouragement. If we are going after something we really want, we must not listen. We must be like Henry the frog and continue upward. This is the way leaders are born and the world changes for the better.

Sharks are concerned only with their own survival and not about other sea life. They do not put the needs of others ahead of themselves. They do not depend on others for survival. They are responsible for their lives from day one. Most of the time, they swim alone.

As parents, once our kids start to become more independent, we must butt out and let them do things on their own. Not doing so will ultimately negatively affect their self-esteem. I know that this can be hard, because we don't want to see them fail, or be made fun of, or get hurt. But allowing them to sink or swim without jumping in and saving them all the time makes them stronger and more resilient.

My daughter Chrissie has always had a mind of her own. When she first started to pick out her own clothes, I was amazed at the outrageous combinations she would put together. Her taste was definitely different from the other kids her age. Knowing my daughter's temperament, I didn't say anything about her unique taste in clothes. But one day, she started to sport a new hairstyle. I don't exactly know what to call it, except that it looked like a water hose exploded on top of her head. She pulled her hair up into a ponytail and sprayed it so it spiked up and fanned out in all directions. I had to say something! She glared at me and said, "It's my hair, and I like it. It makes me look taller. I don't care what anyone else thinks." And off she went.

I was sure that this radical style would only last one day, but I was wrong. Day after day, week after week went by, and she still had the same hairdo before going to school. I could only imagine what her friends were saying behind her back.

Then one day her volleyball team was playing against a rival school. Three moms approached me and went on and on about what a great player Chrissie was and how much their daughters admired her. When they pointed out their daughters to me, these little girls had the same hose coming out of the top of their heads! One player on the other team even wore her hair like Chrissie. I was amazed!

If you dare to be different and have good self-esteem, you can change the world, or at least three little girls on a volleyball court. My daughter didn't care what the other little girls said or thought. Instead, she unknowingly started a fad.

Approval-seekers place a high importance on how they think others feel about them. We need to know how we feel about ourselves, independent of others. This is true self-esteem, and it will drive not only our behaviors, but could actually change society. Do you remember a time when sports were male- dominated and women were shunned and discriminated against for wanting to participate? I do.

Most of my girlfriends became cheerleaders in high school. They were the popular girls on campus and envied by the ones that weren't chosen for the cheerleading squad. But I never wanted to be a cheerleader. I wanted to be the one they were cheering for. I joined the basketball and the volleyball teams and was proud to be able to play sports and represent the school. But we didn't have any crowd supporting us and definitely no cheerleaders. That was for the boys' teams.

If you were a girl playing a sport in high school, you were considered a tomboy or a misfit, right up there with the geeks. After all, the men had the athletic futures in college and professional sports. For women, it was a dead end. We weren't taken seriously. Little did I know that all this was about to change. There were other trailblazers like me who loved sports so much that we just kept at it.

Title Nine was the beginning of equality for women in sports. It gave women's and girls' athletic programs equal funding with the boys' and men's programs. This was huge! College scholarships and professional sports for women were starting to blossom. A new era was beginning as the term *tomboy* was replaced by *female athlete*. Our numbers were growing, and we never looked back.

Today, girls' and women's sports are so alluring that the most popular girls on campuses are the athletes. Being an athlete is similar to being a celebrity. Women's sports are promoted and televised and have tremendous appeal. Women's teams even have their own cheerleaders, and some of them are boys and men! How's that for radical change?

In many schools, students are taught to think a certain way, memorize endless facts, and always agree with the teacher. Going against the grain and being an original thinker in education is typically not encouraged. Conformity is rewarded with good grades and credentials. At graduation, everyone dresses in the same graduation gowns, wears the same hats, and gets the standard diploma, and if they're lucky, they will get a job that will be an acceptable profession.

Instead of conformity, we should be encouraging people to be different. That is what makes life interesting. Do we really want to be like everyone else? What if we all looked the same, acted the same, and had the same jobs? Would that be stimulating? Would you want to marry someone who is exactly like you? I certainly wouldn't.

We have to be willing to risk public humiliation, to be unique, and go after what we want. The road to your unique self is not crowded. Have the courage to be you. The more authentic we are, the more powerful we become. However, we must be willing to go it alone, against the maddening crowd—just like the shark.

Shark Action Steps

1. What is unique about you?

2. Have you ever considered this to be a powerful force?

3. How can you change the world by utilizing this unique talent, skill, or quality?

4. Are you willing to get away from the maddening crowd to make a difference?

Quotes on Individuality

Strength of numbers is the delight of the timid whereas the valiant in spirit glory in fighting alone.—Gandhi

A man who does not think for himself does not think at all.
—Oscar Wilde

If I'm going to sing like someone else, then I'm not going to sing at all.—Billie Holiday

Shark Sense Fourteen:
Sharks Don't Show Their Age

Human Translation: Enter the Ageless Zone

And in the end, it's not the years in your life that count. It's the life in your years.—Abe Lincoln

I had a student a while back named Donna. She was in her mid-fifties, but you'd never know it. She was a vibrant woman with the cutest smile and the biggest laugh in the world. She came back to school to learn, get in shape, and pursue new interests. Her personality attracted many students, and soon she had more friends than she knew what to do with. She was also a very large woman and said that all the women in her family were heavy. One of her goals was to have a normal-sized casket when she died, since all of her relatives needed the super size.

I thought she was kidding, but then I found out that she had an inoperable brain condition and her time was limited, so I became concerned. She attended three of my fitness classes and worked out harder than most of my young students. Several times I had to tell her to slow down because I was afraid that she was going to drop dead in my class. Donna became somewhat of an icon at school, appearing to get younger every day. She changed her hair, lost weight, and finally graduated with her degree. We were all amazed and delighted with her success.

One day, I received news that Donna's aneurysm ruptured and that she had passed peacefully in her sleep. She'd gone to bed one night and didn't wake up, but I'm sure she did awake in heaven! If there was ever a person that did not let age or infirmities stand in her way, it was this wonderful woman. She showed everyone who knew her how to live an ageless life. And yes, she got a normal-sized casket!

Sharks continue to grow in size with age. There are no other visible signs of the aging process. If you saw a shark coming after you in  the water, you'd be concerned no matter how old the shark was, and rightfully so. In fact, the older sharks are the most dangerous because they have tons of experience! They continue to swim and pursue their goals. Age does not slow them down.

We can also continue to grow, not in size, but in the quality of life, if we enter what I call the "ageless zone." This is a mind state where age has no power over us. We are never too old to learn to achieve or give of ourselves to others. We don't stop living because we get old—we get old because we stop living! Learning something new makes us younger. We need to look at learning as if we were going to live forever. Most people look forward to retiring from stressful jobs only to find that they are unhappy because they can't find anything that stimulates their interest and are afraid to try something new.

Too many seniors get old before their time because they stop being active and interested in life. As long as we are breathing, we can make a difference. Like the shark, we will always be achieving and experiencing something new if we keep moving forward. And remember, you can't get old when you are working at something you love. There is always something to love about life. Keep moving forward and you will find it.

Do you want to know your *real age*? I recommend that my health students go to a website to determine how old they are independent of chronological age. It is a simple assessment that takes a look at physiological and psychological health, along with life choices. Many times, a person is either much older or much younger in their real age than their chronological age. In fact, I had one mother in my class that came back younger than her daughter who had taken the same test.

If you are brave enough to handle the results, take the assessment. It will tell you what is making you older than your years and how to reverse the process. Once you know your real age, you will have the information you need to start getting younger. Go to www.realage. com or purchase the book *Real Age: Are You as Young as You Can Be?* by Michael F. Roizen, MD. I promise that it will make an impact and open your eyes to the real causes of aging.

The following shark action steps are the ABCs of how to enter the ageless zone. I put these together a while back as a simple guide to enjoying life regardless of age. They are simple and powerful and will add life to your years and possibly years to your life.

Shark Action: ABC Steps for Entrance to the Ageless Zone

Appreciate life.

Be open to possibilities.

Challenge yourself.

De-clutter your life and your surroundings.

Expect to live a long, fulfilling life.

Free yourself of the past.

Give what you can to others.

Help people who cannot help themselves.

Increase the beauty in your life.

Judge not!

Kindle positive relationships.

Listen more, talk less.

Move your body whenever you can.

Notice nature and its entire splendor.

Organize your priorities.

Pamper yourself because you deserve it.

Quiet the inner chatter in your mind by developing a simple meditation practice.

Reside in the present moment.

See yourself in others.

Think about all your blessings and give thanks.

Unplug the television and go out and experience life for yourself.

Volunteer for a worthy cause.

Write in a journal everyday events that were positive.

e**X**cuses be gone! You don't need them, and we don't want to hear them.

Yoga practice every day—for flexibility and peace of mind.

Be **Z**any—laugh often, have fun, and take chances. You only live once.

Quotes on Aging

Nobody grows old merely by living a number of years. We grow old by deserting our ideals. Years may wrinkle the skin, but to give up enthusiasm wrinkles the soul.—Samuel Ullman

Never too late, never too bad, never too old, never too sick to start from scratch and begin again.—Bikram Choudhury

Epilogue

The next time you hear someone yell "shark!" when you are in the water, get out as fast as you can. You are no match for a hungry shark. But hopefully you now understand more about their nature. Even though we cannot tame sharks or communicate with them, they can teach us a lot. The fact that we can't tame them tells us something—they don't need to be fixed. They are perfect as they are—these elite hunters of the seas that have survived for over four hundred million years.

I'm not suggesting that we vacate the human qualities of love and compassion and become reactive, unsociable, or reclusive. We can keep our positive human traits and hone in on the shark traits that will help us to improve our lives. The shark exemplifies simplicity and power—the no-nonsense approach to life. Sharks are autonomous, driven, and adapt well to change. We can use these shark traits anytime we need them to move us forward toward our dreams. That's using our *Shark Sense*!

For more information on sharks, visit the Shark Research Institute at www. sharks.org or check out a fun website dedicated to the preservation and study of sharks at www.sharkmansworld.com. For information on shark conservation and how you can make a difference, go to www.wildaid.org.

About the Author

Sharkie Zartman is a full-time professor at El Camino College in Torrance, California. She teaches health, fitness, yoga, volleyball, and boot camp fitness. She is a four-time US national champion in volleyball and a former US National Team member. At UCLA, she was a member of the first national championship team and was named one of twenty-five All-Time Greats at UCLA for women's volleyball.  She was also five-year WPVA beach volleyball professional.

In addition to her athletic accomplishments, she coached El Camino College to nine conference and two state titles and led her Spoilers junior volleyball team to one Volleyball Festival National Championship and three second-place finishes. She is a member of the California Beach Volleyball Hall of Fame, El Camino Athletic Hall of Fame, and the Community College Coaches Hall of Fame.

She has written four books, including *Youth Volleyball: The Guide for Coaches and Parents*, *Yoga for Health and Fitness*, *The Road to Fitness*, and *Fitness and Wellness*.

She has two children, Teri and Chrissie, who also competed in volleyball: Teri at University of California at Irvine, and Chrissie at UCLA. Sharkie and her husband, Pat, live in Hermosa Beach, California, just a stone's throw away from the shore.

For more information on classes and workshops, go to www.sharkiezartman.com.

References

Benchley, Peter. *Shark Life*. New York, NY: Delacorte Press, 2005.

Carroll, Pete. *Win Forever: Live, Work, and Play Like a Champion*. New York, NY: Penguin Group, 2010.

Ferguson, Howard E. *The Edge*. Harrison, Ohio: Getting the Edge Company, 1983.

Hurzeler, Donald J. *Designated for Success*. Malvern, PA: CPCU Society, 2004.

Kalman, Bobbie. *Spectacular Sharks*. New York, NY: Crabtree Publishing Company, 2003.

Katie, Byron. *A Thousand Names for Joy*. New York, NY: Random House, 2007.

Lombardi, Vince. *Motivation Lombardi Style*. Aurora, Illinois: Successories Publishing, 1992.

Machowicz, Richard. *Unleashing the Warrior Within*. New York, NY: Hyperion, 2000.

Pope, Joyce. *1001 Facts About Sharks*. New York, NY: DK Publishing, Inc., 2002.

Wooden, John. *Wooden: A Lifetime of Observation and Reflections On and Off the Court*. New York, NY: McGraw-Hill Books, 1997.